CAIRO'S
STREET
STORIES

Lesley Lababidi

CAIRO'S STREET STORIES

Exploring the City's Statues, Squares, Bridges, Gardens, and Sidewalk Cafés

The American University in Cairo Press
Cairo   New York

Page i, iv: Lion by Alfred Jacquemart on Qasr al-Nil Bridge
Pages ii–iii: Court of Lions, in Andalusia Garden, Saad
        Zaghloul in the background
Page vi: Statue of Soliman Pasha at the Citadel
Page viii: Cairo, looking south from Gezira to Roda Island,
        and Maadi beyond

Photographs by Lesley Lababidi: i, iv–v, vi, viii, x, 4 (all), 5,
7, 9, 14, 16–17, 20, 25 (top), 27, 32, 33, 34, 36, 38 (both), 39,
40 (top), 47, 48, 49, 50, 52, 53, 54, 56, 57, 58, 59, 67, 69, 70,
74, 77 (both), 78, 80, 81, 82 (both), 83 (both), 86, 87, 88, 89,
90 (both), 92, 93, 94 (both), 96, 97, 99 (both), 101, 102, 106,
108, 111, 114, 115, 117, 118, 119, 120, 121 (both), 122 (both),
124, 125, 127 (both), 128, 129, 130, 131, 132, 142; Saadiah
Lababidi: ii–iii, 3, 35, 65 (bottom), 66, 75, 110, 113; Digital
Globe: 2; courtesy of the British Museum: 13; George Fakhry:
22, 26, 31; R. Neil Hewison: 25 (bottom), 44–45; courtesy of
Victor Carazo, Ambassador of Venezuela: 40 (bottom); courtesy
of Albrecht Klenk: 44 (top).

First published in 2008 by
The American University in Cairo Press
113 Sharia Kasr el Aini, Cairo, Egypt
420 Fifth Avenue, New York, NY 10018
www.aucpress.com

Dar el Kutub No. 20271/07
ISBN 978 977 416 153 7

Dar el Kutub Cataloging-in-Publication Data

Lababidi, Lesley
        Cairo's Street Stories: Exploring the City's Statues,
    Squares, Bridges, Gardens, and Sidewalk Cafés / Lesley
    Lababidi.—Cairo: The American University in Cairo
    Press, 2007
        p.   cm.
        ISBN 977 416 153 X
        1. Cairo (Egypt)—description and travel
        I. Title
        916.216

1 2 3 4 5 6 7 8   12 11 10 09 08

Designed by Andrea El-Akshar
Printed in Egypt

Dedicated to
Cairo's traffic police
and
taxi drivers

Contents

Acknowledgments

ONE OF MY FAVORITE EXPRESSIONS is "Wherever you look, there is something to see." And being particularly inquisitive, I like to know everything possible about what I see and my surroundings. Thus the idea for this book began to emerge—"What is Cairo to us?" "How do we use space?" "What is the significance of statues, squares, bridges, gardens, cafés in our daily life?" "How do they connect us with the past?" "What stories are to be told?" This book is the result of four years of research, study, and exploration of Cairo's city-space in an attempt to answer these questions. However, without the support, guidance, and scholarship of Neil Hewison throughout those years, this book would not exist. From the kernel of the idea, Neil encouraged me. I am most grateful for Neil's prodding at critical moments, discussions of important questions, suggestions for revision, clarification of details, and for his patience throughout the entire editing process. Thank you.

During her summer holiday from university and before digital cameras were the norm, my daughter, Saadiah Lababidi, photographed Cairo's public statues at the onset of the project. Although only a few of those first images are within these pages, I am appreciative of the time and energy Saadiah devoted to visually recording each statue, and the laughter we shared. Samir Korayem gave insight into and explanation of Egyptian culture and history, and taught me more than I could ever learn in a library, as well as translating documents and literary works. Dr. Sobhi Sharouni solved the mystery of which artist sculpted the statue at Cairo University, and verified each sculptor of each statue. Jayme Spencer facilitated my research at the American University in Cairo library. I am grateful to the Venezuelan Ambassador H.E. Víctor Carazo for providing information and a photograph for the Simón Bolívar statue.

I wish to thank Abdel Aziz Samy, antiquities conservator, and Marcel Takla, conservator of Coptic ceramics, who guided me through the steps of the restoration process. Thanks to Reem Lababidi and Digital Globe for providing the satellite image of Cairo, as well as to driver Ayman Salah, who developed a keen interest in statues and drove carefully through Cairo's congested streets. My mother, Pollyann, and my sister, Lynn, have been a constant source of support. Friends, particularly Lisa, Silvia, and Americo, and family members encouraged me and I am sincerely grateful.

Thanks to editor Sue Viccars for her hard work and patience as well as to Andrea El-Akshar and Miriam Fahmi at the American University in Cairo Press for their superb design and production of this book.

Most of this book was written on walks around Cairo that allowed me to observe movement in the city. I was struck profoundly by the randomness faced by Cairo traffic policemen and taxi drivers every day they go to work. They, too, have stories. It is to them that *Cairo's Street Stories* is dedicated.

x

Eclectic City

THERE MAY BE NO BETTER WAY to appreciate the vast extent of the city of Cairo than to inch around the circumference of the platform at the top of the Cairo Tower on the island of Gezira. As far as the eye can see from this narrow 360-degree ledge, there is city. A hazy sky gives way to the world's longest river, the Nile, meandering almost parallel to the Muqattam Hills to the east. Only the Nile hosts respite from the ancient and modern, from the stone and sand. Twenty million people encased in a gray concrete sea press in on the few and far green spaces. On first turn, silence. North—east—south—west. The monotonous modern-day traffic drones like the background rhythm of a Sufi *rababa*. Another turn, and the city loosens; beneath layers of the modern pulses the history of a thousand years. Rounding a corner, recognition—below: the lions of Qasr al-Nil Bridge guard Saad Zaghloul's statue; the Nile Needle obelisk affirms its place among the swaying palm trees. East: the Darb al-Ahmar district, the new Al-Azhar Park, and the twin minarets on Bab Zuwayla that rise like arrows pointing toward the massive Citadel complex, whose great walls the city encircles as it climbs the Muqattam Hills. South: a towering apartment complex marks an entrance to the suburbs, to Maadi and, beyond, Helwan. West: Saqqara, clouds casting shadows across the five-thousand-year-old Giza pyramids, no longer isolated as the throbbing city advances. Constant, the Nile flows northward. Observed

The great spinning skirt, the *tannura,* that symbolizes the relationship between earth and sky, sun and stars

Cairo from space

from above, history, culture, time, space—all the colors blur in the textures below, like the *tannura* dancer's twirling skirt.

What is Cairo to us? We glorify Cairo; it is all consuming. We love it or we hate it. We shape it and it reshapes us. We fight with it and tire of it. Cairo requires our opinion. We are citizens encapsulated by society, culture, education, and laws, molded by our opinions of the relationship between—and appreciation of—personal and communal space. We define Cairo

continually, integrating time—past, present, future—with history, people, economy, politics, values, movements, education, and environment. The landscapes, districts, palaces, archaeological sites, mosques, churches, buildings, towers, statues, gardens, streets, and alleyways together hold a rich heritage of human and cultural experience and capture the frenzied energies of daily pursuits and survival. How livable is Cairo?

"Why is it," asks J.B. Jackson, "that we have trouble agreeing on the meaning of landscape? The word is simple enough, and it refers to something which we think we understand; and yet to each of us it seems to mean something different."[1] We interpret our city-space by our culture, perceptions, or feelings toward it. Though we share the same space as the background for our collective and personal experiences, interpretation of city-space is as unique as each individual.

The individual who comes into a city is immediately linked to its infrastructures. Our relationship with the people and patterns of the city through time and across space is significant in connecting and interpreting history, and it changes us. Our ambitions change, our perceptions change. Cairo's centuries of history override everything. What we see, how we interpret our impressions and arrive at conclusions, depends on the context of the culture and society in which we grew up. We experience the intensity of Cairo's past. It overwhelms our senses.

Cairo's streets are like an open history book, threading stories together over the centuries. The richness of these stories evolves through the chronicles of time. Foreigners and invaders came to Egypt to expand and to change the prevailing culture. Rulers of ancient civilizations—Persia, Greece, Rome, Byzantium, and Arabia—molded Egypt to reflect their culture, and the indigenous people adapted accordingly, century after century. Each newcomer expanded on what the ancient Egyptians always knew—the landscape of beauty and blessings. Egypt's poet laureate, Ahmad Shawqi, wrote:

Egypt is a story with which the hand of writers and commentators is never done.
Thereof [is a record of] papyrus, and Psalm, and Torah, and Quran, and Gospel,
And Mena, and Cambyses, and Alexander and the two Caesars, and Salah [al-Din] the Great—
Those men and ages are a treasury; so stir your imagination, and it will bring the key.[2]

Egypt's Awakening at Feast time

4

Last-minute shopping for Santa hats in Cairene traffic

Top: Cairo, the 'City of a Thousand Minarets,' actually has over four thousand

Right: Noon traffic on Qasr al-Aini Street, approaching Midan al-Tahrir

Opposite: The Giza pyramids at sunset

Cairo is an ancient city, a capital city, an oriental city, a tourist city, a commercial city, a religious city, a political city, a European city, a city of pyramids. The city space is timeless and vast, and it is human—a living, breathing, pulsing, unique mass of genes.

Cairo is about multitudes, yet each individual in it is about Cairo. An individual's deepest need is to connect with and respond to the commonality of the city. We judge our daily experiences by how livable Cairo is, how this interaction meets our needs, and how we respond to it by sharing space with millions of other Cairenes with diverse pursuits. Cairo is like meeting all of Egypt in one moment. Egyptians speak of Cairo and Egypt in one word, Masr. Cairo is a city as homogeneous as it is diverse, where East and West meet, tug, and co-exist. It is a city carved from the desert by the Nile, a city of industry, music, cinema, religion, antiquity, and historical repute. Cairo is a city that swells and grows, wave after wave, century after century.

Cairo is a consequence of ancient Egyptian history. The pyramids of Saqqara

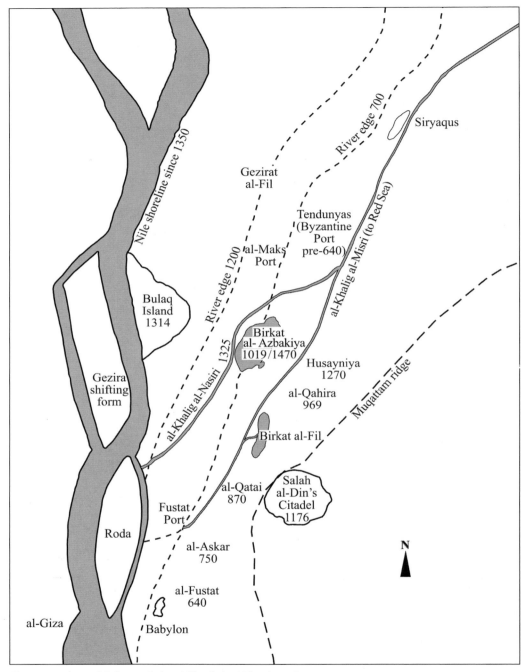

The expansion of Cairo and the shift of the Nile since 640

and Giza, built between 2686 and 2160 BC, stand as testimonials of grandeur and superiority. This monumental message did not go unheeded. Looking westward from Memphis, the capital of the pharaohs, the shimmering pyramids were concrete symbols of the ambitions of the rulers of the country. From the Persian conquest of Memphis in 525 BC, to Trajan, the Roman emperor, in AD 98, to the Arab invasion in 640, to the present, subsequent rulers wanted 'their' cities to equate to the magnitude of the pyramids. As the omni-present Nile flowed to an apex at Memphis connecting the rich Nile Valley to the Mediterranean, control over these waters meant control of Egypt.

Looking east from Al-Azhar Park across the City of the Dead to Manshiyat Nasir

Cairo is...an 'Ahwa

The Fatimid city of al-Qahira was founded in the tenth century AD as an élite twin to the existing city of Fustat. Fustat was a commercial city, a port city, a city for the masses. Al-Qahira was a dynastic city, a palatial city, a city for royalty. Nine hundred years later Ismail Pasha launched a campaign of modernization and transformed the capital. The new addition, Ismailiya—from Qasr al-Aini to Azbakiya—rivaled European cities, but the old Islamic city from Bab al-Hadid to the Citadel to Sayyida Zaynab Square was abandoned to the poor and middle-class masses. Cairo endures and embraces duality; so it is with coffee in the city.

A tradition of drinking tea and coffee in Cairo's 'ahwas, or coffee houses, remains tightly adhered to: black tea with sugar or mint, and thick, strong coffee with sugar in varying degrees—both with the indispensable *shisha*. On the other side of the coin, the western-style 'coffee shops' experiment: café au lait, cappuccino, Earl Grey, tea with milk. Here then lies the duality: 'ahwa—delightfully traditional; coffee shop—conveniently flexible.

8

Ibrahim's coffee house, early 1900s

In every Cairo neighborhood there is an *'ahwa*. Space is rarely a problem. It does not require much to make one: a stove to boil water, a fire for charcoal, an alleyway or sidewalk sufficient for table and chairs. Middle-aged and male-dominated, visible and local, poor to middle-class, a real *'ahwa* is best found in Sayyida Zaynab, Bulaq, or around the Citadel. Many have no names, no signs, just Ibrahim's Place, and definitely no menus. There is a rhythm that moves to the sound of the hubbly-bubbly water-pipe; the *rayyis* takes the order and yells, "'Ahwa mazbout!" The backgammon box comes out. "Shay kushari!" The flickering television blares an Ahli game, tables fill with taxi drivers and shopkeepers for the evening. An *'ahwa* of 250 years (al-Fishawi), or eighty years (al-Hurriya), or a corner coffee house—all are testimonial to the traditional Egyptian style of relaxation.

A coffee house in Ahmad Maher Street

The Cairo coffee shop is for the affluent. Prices are high and the décor is expensive. Waiters are trained to serve with a smile, jotting down the order on paper that reappears as the check with service charge and tax. The menu is in English and Arabic, an array of luxury, flavored coffee and tea with sweets, salads, and sandwiches. Cairo's coffee shop is a recent phenomenon that first appeared in the late 1990s, rapidly spreading within a few years throughout the affluent neighborhoods. The coffee shop is a retreat behind walls and off the street that offers public space for the young, for women and men, for professionals—all who seek a distinctive place to belong. Following a western model, the coffee-shop-goers not only connect experientially with their global counterparts but also connect through wireless Internet.

Yet the line of demarcation is clear, whether between Fatimid twin cities, between the old city and Ismail's new city, or between the *'ahwa* and the coffee shop. Society and relaxation observe economic rules.

River City

ANY DISCUSSION ABOUT CAIRO begins with the Nile, *al-bahr*—the Arabic word for sea. The Nile waters enabled people to develop civilizations along its banks for millennia. The Nile swelled during the summer heat, fertilizing its valley and delta with 140 million tons of rich silt from Aswan to the Mediterranean Sea. Until the construction of the Aswan High Dam in 1970, the river played an important role in communication between Upper and Lower Egypt, served as the highway to transport minerals, grains, and materials, and enriched the land with rich silt for bountiful harvests. Without the African waters there could be no farms to support settlements and civilizations. Herodotus expressed this ancient truth when he wrote in the fifth century BC the now famous words, "Egypt is a gift of the Nile."

Songs of happiness and hope and poetry reverberate with the fidelity and generosity of the river's constant flow. On the walls of the pharaohs' tombs the ancient Egyptians depicted every aspect of life along the banks of the Nile. They recorded animals, birds, fish, and plants, as well as events associated with the flooding of the river's waters revealed in daily and yearly cycles. They were experts in devising elaborate irrigation and agricultural systems to counter the arid climate and benefit from the annual flood. Historians have discovered descriptions of gardens in the palaces of Hatshepsut, Thutmose III, and Akhenaten.

The Khalig al-Misri in the late nineteenth century, before it was filled in to form Port Said Street

Great civilizations flourished and receded as did the Nile waters, leaving remnants of their cultures in our space today. The pharaohs, Persians, Greeks, Romans, Christians, Arabs, and Ottomans agreed, at least, on this one point—the Nile waters sustained life. They built tombs, monuments, and fortifications. Their markets and cities thrived along its banks. Prosperity determined by the abundance or scarcity of the harvest depended on the height of the annual flood. Each year the pharaohs and their successors measured the level of the Nile waters by a stone device called a Nilometer. As the waters rose, the following season's harvests were secured; people and rulers rejoiced, creating festivals to give thanks to the Nile.

The ancient Egyptians believed they lived in a land in which they were blessed; the rising of the sun and the flooding of the Nile translated into rituals recognizing the cycle of life and death. The river was their lifeline and they relished the rhythmic renewal. This inherent relationship continues today as modern Egyptians recognize the Nile's water as a constant source of life, creativity, and development. On a weekend night along the bridges of Cairo wedding parties emerge from cars and taxis to crowd around the newly married couples and take photographs with the Nile flowing beneath their feet: a tradition that is said to bless the marriage in fortune and fertility.

The Romans conquered Egypt in 30 BC and were soon to acknowledge Egypt as the breadbasket of their empire. Emperor Trajan (r. AD 98–117) recognized the strategic geographic position of trade routes from Heliopolis to Memphis, and rebuilt the fortress walls of Babylon on the east bank of the Nile just south of modern Cairo. He also re-excavated a silted-up canal from the Nile to the Red Sea, originally dug by the pharaoh Neko II. As the Nile moved westward, and after five hundred years of silting, Amr ibn al-As again re-cut the canal (in Arabic, al-Khalig al-Misri).

A yearly festival was held called the 'cutting of the dam.' Each year, as the flood waters swelled in the river, a dam was constructed across the entrance to the canal at the point still today called Fumm al-Khalig, 'mouth of the canal,' opposite the southern tip of Roda Island. When the water reached the right height, the dam was ceremonially demolished to allow the waters to flow over the parched land and renew lakes and ponds. Fatimid caliphs, Mamluk sultans, and Ottoman beys gathered to perpetuate the tradition in splendid ceremonies to display the power and glory of their regimes. During Fatimid times the area around the Khalig was open, with gardens, belvederes, and promenades. The Ayyubids and Mamluks improved the area around the banks of the Khalig and divided it into small plots sold for religious or government interests. Housing, markets, and small gardens developed. The broad *midan* of Azbakiya,

Garden scene from the tomb of a Theban nobleman, Nebamun, c. 1400BC. Sycomore fig trees, dom palms, date palms, and mandrake bushes surround a pond teeming with life

which became a lake after the cutting of the dam, was utilized for recreational purposes.

With centuries of use, the waterway beyond the city played an important role in the growth of villages, providing a well-marked route for locals, foreigners, and invaders, and aided the development of commerce, agriculture, and communication. Rulers and dynasties, one after another, dipped their hands in the powerful Nile, diverting its water to create the city they envisioned for themselves and leaving the ever-growing population to settle along the periphery.

Virgin City
640–1270

EACH RULING DYNASTY LEFT ITS MARK by reflecting a unique vision for their society. They were architects of a virgin space and used the environment to fulfill their needs and express their beliefs. The Umayyads brought Islam to the Byzantine province of Egypt in the seventh century. From Damascus, Caliph Umar sent his commander Amr ibn al-As and an army of fifteen thousand men; they arrived at a small port on the Nile, the Byzantine stronghold of Tendunyas (also known as Umm Dunain, and later under the Fatimids as al-Maks). There a battle raged, and the Byzantine army was defeated. Amr ibn al-As encamped at the city of Heliopolis, which he renamed Ain Shams, and continued on to the Roman fortress of Babylon. It was here, on the strategic eastern bank of the Nile, that Amr ibn al-As settled in 642. The encampment he established, al-Fustat, was twenty kilometers south of the Delta, and across the river from the ancient capital of Memphis, at the point where the Muqattam Hills meet the Nile. The first Arab city in Egypt, al-Fustat developed spontaneously.

The River Nile was the single factor that gave al-Fustat life. With the reopening of the canal, the Umayyads used the waterways to communicate between Arabia, al-Fustat, and Upper Egypt. Their main goal was to expand Islam, but they also advanced the concept of the garden from its origins in Persian, Roman, and Byzantine cultures. Courtyards in living spaces and public areas were in use well before the rise of

The Nile in Cairo, looking south, with the Abbas Bridge and the Munib Bridge beyond

15

Islam, providing shade and privacy, as were the gardens of the Roman fortress; while in monasteries, monks planted their gardens for beauty and subsistence. Courtyards and gardens in private houses gave protection from the hot, dry desert climate.

A power struggle began between the Umayyads and the Abbasids of Baghdad for the control of the Islamic empire, and to rule Egypt. The Abbasids founded a new princely city, al-Askar ('the troops'), northeast of al-Fustat in 750. Al-Askar became the second Islamic capital of Egypt, a well-planned city with facilities (of which there is no trace today) to support the new ruling elite and military troops. This left al-Fustat as a port, a growing commercial district—unplanned and with poor facilities—and home to ordinary Egyptians.

Ahmad Ibn Tulun arrived from Baghdad in 868 as governor of Egypt. He began his own program of expansion and, in refusing to send the annual tribute to the Abbassid caliph, broke ties with Baghdad and proceeded to rule Egypt independently. In 870 he built his city to the northeast of al-Fustat and al-Askar and named it al-Qatai ('the wards,' or allotments of land parcels similar to the quarters in his native Samarra). Ibn Tulun constructed his mosque in the Samarra tradition as a token of remembrance, with a spiraling minaret.

During the eighth century, the Nile changed course to define four islands—Roda, Gezira, Bulaq, and al-Fil, the latter two of which later became part of the eastern mainland. As the waters shifted, there were floods at Amr ibn al-As Mosque in al-Fustat. Over ten years, sediment built along the east banks, resulting in a westward shift of the Nile that left the land, the mosque, and the Babylon fortress dry. The rich sediment produced fertile ground where, eventually, luxurious gardens grew in the midst of palatial residences in and around al-Qatai. Al-Fustat and al-Askar fused together as a trade and commerce center to support this new royal city, which developed around the mosque of Ibn Tulun, each quarter identified according to ethnicity and/or government standing. Ibn Tulun incorporated a hospital (probably one of few in the world at that time) and an administrative building, and built an aqueduct to bring water from the Nile to a hippodrome or *midan* for parades and polo games and botanical gardens. Historian Doris Behrens-Abouseif writes: "Ibn Tulun's son Khumarawayh . . . took special care of the garden of rare flowers and trees. Tree trunks were coated with gilded copper from which pipes trickled water into canals and fountains to irrigate the garden, and nearby was an aviary with singing birds. Most remarkable was a pool of mercury, where Khumarawayh, an insomniac, lay on an air mattress trying to rock himself to sleep. The entire complex, with its gardens, huge stables and menagerie of wild animals, did not overlook the Nile but rather the Birkat al-Fil, a large pond connected to the Khalij. In the surrounding area, luxury markets soon sprang up to serve the tastes of officers and notables."[3]

Change would again transform the landscape, as from Ifriqiya (present-day Tunisia) came the Shi'ite Fatimids under the command of General Jawhar the Sicilian. Following the orders of the caliph al-Muizz li-Din Allah, Jawhar laid plans for a new walled city to the north, once again, where fresh northern winds prevailed. In 969 the Fatimids named their city al-Qahira—'the victorious'—Cairo.

The caliph and the élite entourage remained in elegant palaces behind the walls of this royal city, while outside its gates al-Fustat continued to develop into a vibrant commercial industrial area and port. "Travelers visiting [al-Fustat] from the tenth to the mid-eleventh centuries reported that it competed in grandeur and prosperity with the greatest Islamic cities of the time. Al-Muqaddasi in the tenth century described the high-rise buildings of al-Fustat as resembling minarets. According to Nasiri Khusraw, a Persian traveler of the early eleventh century, some of these buildings climbed as high as fourteen stories up to roof gardens complete with ox-drawn water wheels for irrigating them."[4] Al-Qahira and al-Fustat remained dual cities for nearly two centuries. Al-Qahira was a fortified palace compound created specifically for the Fatimid caliph, his royal court, and his army. Between the palaces lavish gardens flourished, and the Fatimids docked their naval ships at the ancient Roman port-city of Tendunyas,

which they named al-Maks. Al-Fustat was the densely populated commercial port and industrial center of the common people.

In the twelfth century Nur al-Din, the Sunni ruler of Syria, determined to realign Egypt with its Sunni past. Recognizing Egypt as key in the fight against the invading Crusaders, and despite the fact that Cairo was still under weak Fatimid rule, Nur al-Din sent his army to Egypt and appointed Salah al-Din vizier in 1167. Soon after, through a series of cunning administrative directives, Salah al-Din (better known as Saladin in the west) was able to overturn Fatimid rule and become *de facto* ruler of Egypt, taking the title of *sultan*—'the holder of authority.' In 1171 Salah al-Din began to repair the disintegrating Fatimid walls of al-Qahira, and in 1176, again recognizing the advantage of building northward, he constructed a citadel at the rise of the Muqattam Hills, strategically and without subtlety dominating Cairo, as the monumental pyramids had done for millennia.

The new Citadel housed Salah al-Din's government and his military slaves—*Mamluks*—imported from the Caucasus. Al-Qahira and al-Fustat evolved in opposite directions: the former developed, while the latter declined. Meanwhile, Salah al-Din's Citadel towered over al-Qahira, a constant symbol of the formidable rulers that were to come in future centuries.

During the Ayyubid period (ushered in by Salah al-Din), the city remained densely populated and compact, yet expanded

18

steadily in all directions. Ibn Jubayr, a Moor from Spain, wrote during his visit to Cairo in 1183: "On the west bank of the Nile, which runs between the two [cities], is a large and important burgh with fine buildings called al-Jizah [Giza]. Every Sunday it holds a large market where many congregate. Between it and Misr [Cairo] is an island [Roda] with fine houses and commanding belvederes, which is a resort for entertainment and diversion."[5]

Public gardens were not easily maintained unless near the Nile or the canal; otherwise an irrigation system was necessary with cisterns and waterwheels, which was expensive and thus enjoyed only by the élite. The canals and the yearly flooding of the Nile that produced the ponds in low areas were paramount in creating pleasure gardens and shady respite in a hot climate.

As early as the ninth century, the Abbasid caliphs took slaves from Turkey and surrounding areas. They were trained as soldiers and converted to Islam. These slave-soldiers were intensely loyal to the sultan, and many Mamluks (literally, 'owned') rose to high positions, although their children could not inherit their status. Each new recruit received the same intense training to ensure the continuity of the military order. In 1249 the Mamluks overthrew their Ayyubid masters and proceeded to rule Egypt for more than 250 years, during which time they expelled the Mongols from Syria and stopped the advancing Crusader army. The Mamluks

kept strictly within their caste and mainly spoke Turkish. They continued the separation between rulers and populace; the common people were barred from the military corps, denying them any chance for advancement into the ruling élite.

Nevertheless, for the whole of the Mamluk period Cairo witnessed a flowering of superb art and architecture, and construction and urbanization that Egypt had not seen since the time of Alexander the Great and the Ptolemies (332–30 BC).

Cairo, looking west: Giza Pyramids (horizon), Giza Zoo (left), Cairo University (center), *Egypt's Awakening* (lower center), Orman Botanical Garden (right)

Medieval City
1270–1517

FROM THE FATIMID CITY WALLS to Salah al-Din's Citadel, Cairo filled in and spread out to the north. The Nile receded to the west, exposing Gezirat al-Fil ('Elephant Island') and silting up the port of al-Maks; a new port was created at Bulaq. In 1270 Baybars I built a massive congregational mosque and palace in the Husayniya district, which developed quickly as wealthy merchants settled around the palace. The population spread out along the city's northern wall. To the west, the expansion developed along the Khalig al-Misri and on the island of Roda. Sixty years later, Sultan al-Nasir Muhammad opened a new canal that branched from the Nile and ran parallel to the Cairo Canal. Named al-Khalig al-Nasiri, it brought water to the north of al-Qahira and the village of Siryaqus (now al-Khankah), where the sultan had his pavilion for hunting and polo. The sultan then opened up the land between the two canals for settlement, abolishing taxes in the area to encourage market growth, and it soon filled with orchards, elegant mansions, and mosques.

Two types of city-space that were highly valued by the Ayyubids and the Mamluks were the *midan* (a polo field or hippodrome, used for military exercise and horseman-ship) and the *bustan* (a Persian word signifying a large garden or orchard). *Midans*, according to Nasser Rabat, "became essential urban spaces in Cairo, . . . as everywhere else in the Islamic world where Turkic horsemen ruled. . . .

The Citadel, with the Mosque of Muhammad Ali, built in 1830, overlooks Midan al-Qal'a (formerly Midan al-Rumayla)

They were royal establishments for polo games and equestrian exercises, the backbone of the Mamluk military organization." Al-Midan al-Kabir, today known as Midan al-Qal'a, beneath the Citadel and cornered by the Sultan Hassan Mosque on its northwestern side, is Cairo's only remaining Mamluk *midan*, of eight that once existed. The great medieval *bustans* have disappeared under the changing structure of the city in the intervening centuries. Their memory, Nasser Rabat tells us, "is preserved primarily in the *waqf* [endowment] documents of buildings that were erected on their sites and in the accounts of literati, who describe many festive settings in them with ceremonial, recreational, literary, or amorous aims.

From these descriptions emerges an image of verdant gardens with both decorative and fruit trees and some light pavilions scattered across the landscape."[6]

Between 1300 and 1500, as the Mamluks brought stability and security to the eastern Mediterranean after the wars of the Crusades, merchants from Syria and Egypt traveled to Europe, particularly Venice, with textiles, spices, and delicacies from the east, and a counterflow of commerce and travelers from Europe reached Mamluk lands. Commerce in grain and trade from the spice route used Cairo's new port on the Nile at Bulaq. From the port to the city, caravanserais and places for lodging expanded to meet the needs of the travelers.

The Citadel and Midan al-Rumayla at the end of the eighteenth century, during the French occupation

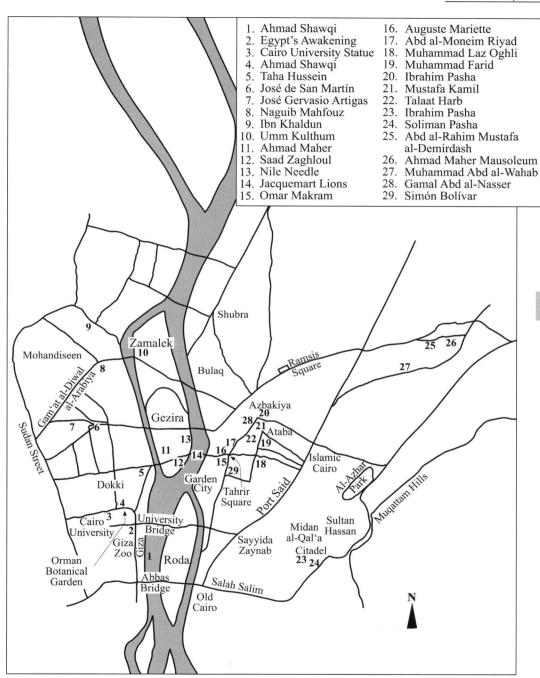

1. Ahmad Shawqi
2. Egypt's Awakening
3. Cairo University Statue
4. Ahmad Shawqi
5. Taha Hussein
6. José de San Martín
7. José Gervasio Artigas
8. Naguib Mahfouz
9. Ibn Khaldun
10. Umm Kulthum
11. Ahmad Maher
12. Saad Zaghloul
13. Nile Needle
14. Jacquemart Lions
15. Omar Makram
16. Auguste Mariette
17. Abd al-Moneim Riyad
18. Muhammad Laz Oghli
19. Muhammad Farid
20. Ibrahim Pasha
21. Mustafa Kamil
22. Talaat Harb
23. Ibrahim Pasha
24. Soliman Pasha
25. Abd al-Rahim Mustafa al-Demirdash
26. Ahmad Maher Mausoleum
27. Muhammad Abd al-Wahab
28. Gamal Abd al-Nasser
29. Simón Bolívar

Cairo and its statues

At the height of this period of prosperity, in 1382, the great historian and philosopher Ibn Khaldun traveled from Tunis to Egypt en route to the *hajj*, the pilgrimage to Mecca. When he arrived in Cairo, the Mamluk sultan Barquq, impressed with Ibn Khaldun's scholarship, offered him a position; he remained in Cairo for three years, teaching (the Egyptian historian al-Maqrizi was a student of his). Dazzled by the city and its people, Ibn Khaldun writes that he "beheld the city of the universe, the orchard of the world, the thronging-place of the nations and anthill of the human race; . . . embellished with palaces and pavilions, ornamented with khanqahs and madrasas, illumined by the moons and stars of its learned men. . . . I wandered the streets of the city filled with passing throngs, its markets crammed with good things, and we continued to remark upon this metropolis, its far stretches of flourishing constructions and its expansive condition."[7] In another passage, Ibn Khaldun offers us an insight into another side of Cairo, the city of the masses: "The commonest cause of epidemics is the pollution of the air resulting from a denser population which fills it with corruption and dense moisture. . . . That is why we mentioned, elsewhere, the wisdom of leaving open empty spaces in built-up areas, in order that the winds may circulate, carrying away all the corruption produced in the air by animals and bringing in its place fresh, clean air."[8] Since the reign of

24

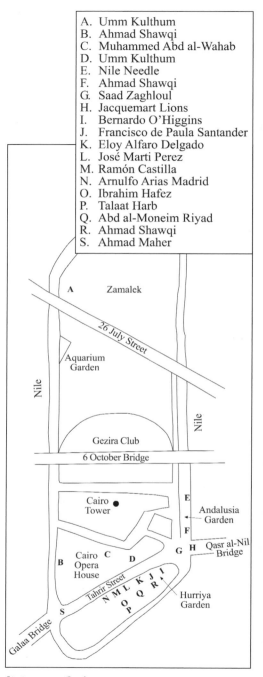

A. Umm Kulthum
B. Ahmad Shawqi
C. Muhammed Abd al-Wahab
D. Umm Kulthum
E. Nile Needle
F. Ahmad Shawqi
G. Saad Zaghloul
H. Jacquemart Lions
I. Bernardo O'Higgins
J. Francisco de Paula Santander
K. Eloy Alfaro Delgado
L. José Marti Perez
M. Ramón Castilla
N. Arnulfo Arias Madrid
O. Ibrahim Hafez
P. Talaat Harb
Q. Abd al-Moneim Riyad
R. Ahmad Shawqi
S. Ahmad Maher

Statues on Gezira

Ibn Khaldun
in Mohandiseen, in Mamluk attire

history, the *Kitab al-i'bar.* After a lifetime of travel, observation, and scholarly works that established him as the founder of modern history, sociology, and economics, Ibn Khaldun died and was buried in Cairo in 1406, probably near Bab al-Nasr, although his tomb is unmarked.

A concrete bust of Ibn Khaldun stands in Midan Ibn Khaldun, next to Ibn Khaldun School on Mahrusa Street in Mohandiseen. It was first erected in January 1962 in front of the National Center for Sociological and Criminal Research, but in 2001 it was moved across the street to an adjacent square, restored as a garden to celebrate Giza National Day.

The ancestors of Abu Zayd Abd al-Rahman Ibn Muhammad **Ibn Khaldun** al-Hadhrami (1332–1406) arrived on the Iberian Peninsula from Yemen. After nearly a century in Seville they left for Tunis, where Ibn Khaldun was born, when the Christians conquered the area. When he was in his late teens the Black Death struck his family, killing his parents and many of his teachers. He moved to Morocco looking for a position in government, which he secured, but then became deeply embroiled in political intrigues. It is through Ibn Khaldun's autobiography that we have the opportunity to relive the political and religious turmoil and conspiracies of the time.

Sometime between 1375 and 1379 Ibn Khaldun settled in the Castle of Ibn Salama in Algeria, where he devoted himself to his passion for study and wrote the famous *Muqaddima (Introduction)* to his book of

Ibn Khaldun on Boulevard Bourguiba in Tunis, as teacher and scholar

the Fatimid ruler al-Hakim bi-Amr Illah, refuse had been discarded on mounds around the city; by the time of Ibn Khaldun's visit these mounds had become mountains of garbage (one of which forms the basis of the beautifully landscaped rolling hills of today's Al-Azhar Park).

Mamluk sultans encouraged their amirs to construct their mansions and monuments in new areas. A typical foundation was a tomb complex: a mosque–mausoleum, a theological school (*madrasa*), with a Sufi hostel (*khanqah*) and sometimes a charitable hospital or a water fountain (*sabil*) attached. The construction of these monuments served to perpetuate the owner's glory in the present and the hereafter, and also stimulated economic growth.

As the city expanded there was a conceptual shift in the utilization of space. The ruling class began to look inward, and the architecture mirrored that change. Their residential palaces incorporated gardens within immense courtyards, rather than facing outward. The sultan distributed the open land to his amirs, who built their large houses on it. These normally included a *maq'ad*, an open rectangular room on the first floor overlooking the garden or courtyard, which often incorporated a fountain or water pool. The courtyard functioned as a private garden where the family turned for protection from the heat and dust and for privacy; open terraces were part of the architecture, so the occupants could appreciate greenery without being in a public

Azbakiya as it appeared at the end of the eighteenth centry

Azbakiya is the only green space in downtown Cairo today

place. As a result any available city space came to be used for public activities rather than for leisurely pursuits.

In 1470 the amir Azbak al-Tutush, a general of sultan Qaitbay, selected the site for his tomb complex and palace on the edge of an open area. Five hundred years earlier, the Fatimids had used the land as a plantation, Bustan al-Maksi, but in 1019 the trees were removed to make way for a large pond.[9] Over the years, the pond filled with silt and was eventually abandoned. The amir saw the potential of the area and had the pond re-excavated; henceforth, during the annual inundation, it filled with waters from the Khalig al-Nasiri at the cutting of the dam. Wealthy merchants followed Azbak and built their splendid villas on the banks of the lake. By the time the Ottomans arrived in Egypt in 1517, Birkat al-Azbakiya was the most fashionable area in Cairo.

Oriental City
1517–1801

DURING THE OTTOMAN ERA, from 1517 to 1798, expansion continued along the same lines (with respect to the Nile's seasonal floods) and urban development continued in the same direction as under the Mamluks. After the Ottoman invasion of 1517, Europeans began to travel to the city of a thousand stories, among them probably the French orientalist Guillaume Postel, who wrote his *Descriptio* in 1549. This description of the city inspired the Venetian printer and cartographer Mateo Pagano to engrave a Renaissance view of Cairo. Though Pagano had never traveled to Egypt, he mapped the city with extraordinary accuracy from an imaginary aerial view from the text of Postel's *Descriptio*. The map's visual representation of the city, its landscape, and its cultural events were the main source of information relied upon by western scholars of the time. For the first time topographical information about Cairo had been relayed to Europe, and thus the western interpretation of the city would remain for the next two centuries until the French Expedition of 1798.[10]

Under the Ottomans, Egypt became a mere province of a great empire, subject to the sultan in Istanbul. But trade with Europe grew, with Bulaq serving as the commercial port. Wealthy merchants and families associated with the ruling class constructed elegant mansions not only around Birkat al-Azbakiya but also in the districts of Nasiriya (near Sayyida Zaynab) and Birkat al-Fil, the former

Cairo as mapped in the *Description de l'Egypte*, at the end of the eighteenth century

island of Gezirat al-Fil, now part of the mainland. In 1670 John Ogilby wrote: "From Bulaq to Grand Cairo the land is all flat, and the way very pleasant, being much frequented with travelers; but the most beautiful part is a place called Usbechia [Azbakiya] in the suburbs, near the city gate; this Usbechia is a round piece of land, encompassed about with houses, which yield a prospect infinitely pleasant, not only when the fields are decked with flowers, but also when by the recess of the Nile, it seems like a drained pond, full of various forms of living fishes."[11] Nevertheless, for the common people, the years were turbulent. Pestilence and famine were constant threats, as was political instability as one foreign ruler after another vied to control Egypt.

In 1768 some of the remaining Mamluks, who had once again become a military force in Egypt, overthrew the Ottomans. Four years later, the Ottoman army re-established imperial authority, and the Mamluks continued to wrest or lose more or less power until 1798, when Napoleon Bonaparte and a large French Republican army invaded Egypt. Bonaparte's mission included an interest in the ancient civilization, but the main purpose of the invasion was to open a route between France and India before the British could do so. Egypt's Isthmus of Suez was the meeting place of three continents: Africa, Asia, and the 'liquid continent' of the Mediterranean, and the importance of control of this vital fulcrum was not lost on the major powers.

If it were not for Napoleon and the artists and scientists who accompanied his invading army we would not know Egypt as we do today. On 19 May 1798 General Bonaparte and his army of nearly fifty thousand men set sail from Toulon, France. In the party was an élite entourage of savants, including architects, mathematicians, astronomers, civil engineers, draftsmen, artists, and printers. Having evaded the British navy in the Mediterranean, the French fleet arrived at Alexandria on 1 July, and Napoleon marched half his army south to Cairo in the grueling summer heat. A short distance outside Cairo one of the Mamluk rulers, Murad Bey, mustered a full force of seven thousand men mounted on the finest Arabian horses and attacked the French on 21 July. At what was to be known as the Battle of the Pyramids, Bonaparte and his generals waged a two-hour battle in which their troops virtually annihilated five thousand Mamluks, the remainder fleeing to Upper Egypt. After the battle Napoleon commented: "Could I have united the Mamluk horse to the French infantry, I would have reckoned myself master of the world."[12] Bonaparte took advantage of the routing of the Mamluks and confiscated their mansions and palaces throughout the city. In the district of Azbakiya he set up his headquarters on the western shore of the lake in the palace of al-Alfi Bey. (Later, in 1841, this same palace was to become Samuel Shepheard's New British Hotel.)

The palace of al-Alfi Bey, Napoleon's headquarters in Cairo

By September 1798 an Ottoman army engaged Napoleon's troops in Syria, and after an unsuccessful attempt to control Acre and Tripoli the French retreated and the Ottoman troops advanced toward Egypt. When they attempted to land at Abu Qir the French army defeated them but, finally abandoning interest in his Egyptian campaign, Napoleon Bonaparte handed command of the army to General Kléber and left for France in August 1799. French troops held on to Egypt until 1801, when the British army under Generals Abercrombie and Hutchinson ousted the French, leading to a power vacuum that the competing Mamluks and Ottomans failed to fill. But serving with the Ottoman army was a young Albanian deputy commander, Muhammad Ali. By 1803 Muhammad Ali had successfully risen in the ranks, and within only three more years had estab-lished enough personal power and control over the Mamluks to have himself appointed governor or *wali* of Egypt by the Ottoman sultan. His heirs would rule Egypt until 1952.

Napoleon Bonaparte did not realize his dream of French dominance from Egypt to the East. But the work of the team of scholars who arrived in Egypt with him, the Commission of Arts and Sciences, through their detailed exploration of the Nile Valley led to birth of the modern discipline of Egyptology. Between 1809 and 1822 the wealth of material collected during the French occupation was turned into a master-piece publication, the *Description de l'Egypte*, consisting of reams of descriptive text and more than three thousand illustrations. It illuminated an academic voyage into the Orient and antiquity that opened explorers' hearts and adventurers' imaginations.

Cairo is...a *Gineina*

Pots of cacti on a window's edge; statues wreathed in greenery on busy roundabouts; city bridges lined with white plastic chairs expectant of the evening crowds; the sloping hills of Al-Azhar Park along the Ayyubid wall—how we react to and interact with these images, whether a statue from another generation or a garden carved from a medieval garbage dump, depends on how we define the space we move in.

The city reflects human needs and esthetic values in how space is used. Green space in Cairo is defined by the diversity of the living spaces of its population: the crowded red-brick districts juxtaposed against the modern high-rise buildings alongside the fast-disappearing villas. Cairo is a city carved from the desert, an oasis along the Nile waters. Traditionally, for the ruling class, a green, open space was to be found in garden-palaces beyond the city walls; for the peasants, it was in land to irrigate and cultivate for agricultural use. Parks and gardens fit into the city's historical fabric, arising from the gardens of palaces (like the Orman Botanical Garden), from the banks of the Nile (the Andalusia Garden), or from a revitalization of urban space (the Al-Azhar Park).

The Arabic words for parks and gardens give us an insight into the importance of green, open spaces. *Roda*, meaning garden or meadow, is perceived as a large area filled with flowers and fruit trees. *Bustan*, Persian for garden or orchard, comes from *bu*, meaning aroma, and *stan*, meaning place: we can imagine a place full of fragrances. In the Quran, the Garden of Paradise is *Jannat al-firdaws*, and *ganna* (in the Egyptian pronunciation) is paradise in the common parlance. The diminutive of *ganna*, *gineina* ('little garden') is a commonly used word for gardens in general, particularly smaller ones. *Hadiqa*, often used now for larger gardens or parks, comes from a root meaning 'to enclose.'

With little rain in Cairo, these green spaces owe their existence to the Nile—and to someone in the government who protects public green space from developers. Most

A window garden above a beauty salon in a lane near Bab Zuwayla

The old Semiramis Hotel (built in 1906), from the Andalusia Garden

gardens in Cairo are enclosed by walls or iron fences, have opening hours, and charge an entrance fee that keeps out the poorer strata of society—so for some families in search of open space, a 'garden' can simply be a triangle of grass beside a busy on-ramp, or the sidewalk on a bridge.

Gezira Island was uninhabitable until the mid-nineteenth century because of the annual floods. Ismail Pasha brought engineers in to solve the problem by constructing reinforcements along the banks, and by 1869 the Gezira Palace stood at the center of the island. Around the palace were vast, magnificent gardens, where the royal family could hunt or spend an afternoon at the racecourse or on the polo field. The khedive

The new Semiramis Hotel (background left), from the Andalusia Garden

had a grotto and an aquarium for his and his guests' pleasure, designed by Delchevalerie and built by Combat and Dumpily—and in 1902 the Hadiqat al-Asmak (Aquarium

Garden) was opened to the public, after Captain Stanley Flower spent £1,500 to have it re-landscaped.

At the southern end of Gezira the khedive established the Ismail Garden in 1876. Originally this garden spread over twelve hectares, covering the entire tip of the island, but the Sheraton Gezira Hotel, the Cairo Sporting Club, a small army barracks, a presidential security headquarters, and the Mukhtar Museum have between them whittled its current size down to about two hectares. After the Free Officers Revolution of 1952, the garden's name changed to the Hurriya ('Freedom') Garden. Its shaded areas in symmetrical orientation bring relief from the heat of the day. The tall, old trees soften the sunlight and provide a barrier from the busy Tahrir Street that runs along its northern boundary. Flowers and pruned shrubs add to the beauty, and a sidewalk circles the garden's ten statues: Ahmad Shawqi, Hafez Ibrahim, Talaat Harb, Abd al-Moneim Riyad, and six busts of Latin American liberators.

Across the road to the north is the Opera House, completed in 1988 in cooperation with Japan. The gardens are spacious and elegant, and boast three statues of Egyptian personalities: Umm Kulthum, Muhammad Abd al-Wahab, and Ahmad Shawqi.

Friday afternoon in Al-Azhar Park

A Nubian dance troupe rehearses on Friday afternoon in the Orman Botanical Garden

The Quran (2:25) says: "And convey good news to those who believe and do good deeds that they shall have gardens in which rivers flow." Water is an essential element in an Islamic garden, of which the best examples in Cairo are the Al-Azhar Park and the Andalusia Garden, where water and shade are both fundamental features of the design.

Along the eastern bank of Gezira Island a series of three narrow gardens stretch from Midan Saad Zaghloul to the main entrance of the Gezira Club: the Andalusia Garden, the Arab Garden, and the Pharaonic Garden all have distinctive features that bear out their names. The history of the Andalusia Garden dates back to 1929, when Mahmoud Zulficar Bey, a member of the royal family, designed and landscaped the garden as a gift for his wife. The garden—used as a private roller-skating rink for the royals—was opened to the public in 1935. The charm of a secluded garden lined by shade trees, the essence of nature in geometric patterns, the softness of interlaced arches—the Andalusia Garden (but a daydream of the grand Alhambra paradise garden of al-Andalus) is serenity in the city. Colorful tiles interplay with terraced grasses that balance the unity of the garden. The play of sun and shadow on the benches that surround the courtyard provide privacy and relief from the heat. At the far end of the garden, on either side, are jasmine-covered gazebos surrounding a fountain supported by a court of marble lions. The presence of Ahmad Shawqi's statue—who in a thoughtful pose oversees the garden—is a western influence. The flow of the Nile to the east must suffice the visitor, for the crucial element of a paradise garden is missing: the fountains and pools to mirror the heavens are now dry.

Egyptian City
1801–Today

MOST CIVILIZATIONS UTILIZE monumental figures and heroic sculptures to revere political figures and leaders. The tradition of immortalizing an individual, whether by human representation or by symbol, is a human trait. Governments impress their political heroes and leaders on their public; erecting statues at major intersections and in parks and gardens appears to reinforce both past heroic accomplishments and current ruling dogma. Heroic sculptures and monumental statues are visible reminders of a time in history when these individuals brought about substantial change in society and, in turn, influenced thought.

Ismail Pasha (viceroy, then khedive of Egypt from 1863 to 1879) no doubt took note of statues of rulers—and particularly equestrian statues of English and French kings—on the public squares of Paris and London during his visits in the 1860s. Ismail, Turkish himself (though born in Egypt) and at home in royal courts, was influenced by earlier Ottoman rulers. Sultan Mahmud II (1808–39) sent portraits of himself to all Turkish and Arab provinces. His son, Abdulaziz (1839–61), continued this practice, and was the only Ottoman ruler to commission sculptures. This public display of authority and superiority in representational form impressed the symbolic message that what had gone before must remain grand in the present and grandiose in the future.

A pink granite wing on the Cairo University statue, a pharaonic symbol of protection and liberty

José Gervasio Artigas

In 1979 the Venezuelan first lady, Dona Blanca Rodriguez de Perez, presented a six-foot bronze statue of General **Simón Bolívar** to Egypt in recognition of the latter's struggle for independence from Britain. Bolívar is known in South America as *El Libertador* for his victories over the Spaniards, as he won independence for Bolivia, Colombia, Ecuador, Peru, and Venezuela between 1813 and 1830. Bolívar hoped to form a union of the new South American nations—as Gamal Abd al-Nasser had hoped to unite the Arab countries in the mid-twentieth century—but the accomplishments of neither leader met their aspirations.

Nevertheless, with a count of twelve statues in five continents from China to Austria, from Missouri to Jamaica, and from Colombia to Cairo, Simón Bolívar is one of the most recognized figures in the world. In Cairo his statue commands his eponymous square between Midan al-Tahrir and the Nile. The sculpture is by Bolívar's compatriot, Carmelo Tabaco, on a pedestal designed by Manuel Silveira Blanco. Every year on

José de San Martín

5 July, the Venezuelan Embassy celebrates Bolívar's accomplishments and the country's independence by placing flowers around the statue.

In Mohandiseen, at opposite ends of Mohi al-Din Abu al-Ezz Street, stand the busts of **José Gervasio Artigas** and **José de San Martín**, each in his own square. Artigas, born in Montevideo, was a Uruguayan national hero. He fought first with the Spanish against the British for the liberation of Buenos Aires. His allegiance then shifted, as he led the popular uprising against the Spanish and Portuguese in 1815. He was exiled to Paraguay before Uruguay won its independence. San Martín helped to liberate Argentina, Chile, and Peru from Spanish rule. He met Simón Bolívar in Ecuador in 1815 and each declared himself the liberator of South America—Bolívar of the north, San Martín of the south.

Six more busts of South American liberators are sited in the Hurriya Garden on Gezira Island: **Bernardo O'Higgins**, together with José de San Martín, liberated Chile and became its first independent leader.

From front to back: Bernardo O'Higgins, Francisco de Paula Santander, General Eloy Alfaro Delgado, José Marti Perez, Ramón Castilla

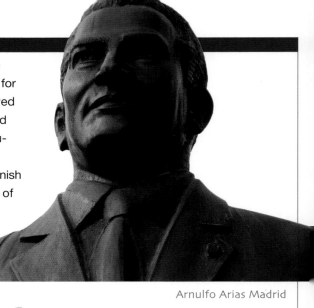

Ramón Castilla originally served in the Spanish army but in 1822 joined the fight for independence with San Martín. He served as president of Peru twice and abolished slavery in the country. Colombian revolutionary **Francisco de Paula Santander** fought with Simón Bolívar against the Spanish and served under him as vice president of Colombia. **Eloy Alfaro Delgado** was twice president of Ecuador, from 1895 to 1901 and from 1906 to 1911. A liberal capitalist, he believed in separation of

Arnulfo Arias Madrid

state and church, freedom of speech, and civil rights; he was brutally killed in 1912. **José Marti Perez** died in the war to liberate Cuba from Spain in 1895. **Arnulfo Arias Madrid**, a Harvard-trained physician, served as president of Panama three times: in 1940–41, 1949–51, and for eleven days in 1968; each time he was deposed by a military coup. During the Second World War he was a keen supporter of European fascism, even using the swastika and the fasces as symbols.

During the nineteenth and twentieth centuries, these men fought for liberation and independence—ideals dear to the hearts of Egyptians.

A typical 5 July in Cairo: Venezuelan Ambassador Víctor R. Carazo and the ambassadors of Colombia, Peru, Panama, and Bolivia, commemorate Simón Bolívar

Ismail's visit to Paris for the Exposition Universelle in 1867 was a catalyst for the transformation of Cairo. Since Muhammad Ali's reign the ruling family had tried to shake off the influence of the Ottoman Empire. Ismail planned to wield power in Egypt and disengage from Istanbul. To create an image of an Egyptian dynasty, he commissioned Charles Henri Cordier and Alfred Jacquemart, respectively, to create equestrian statues of his father, Ibrahim Pasha, and his grandfather, Muhammad Ali (unveiled in Alexandria in 1873). (At the same time other sculptors were promoting peace and unity between Egypt and the Ottomans: Faustin Glavany, a Levantine, displayed a model for a pyramidal monument with four sphinxes at the Exposition Universelle in Paris. The statue was to be placed at the entrance of the Suez Canal, complete with inscriptions for peace between Egypt, Europe (France), and Asia (Turkey) in hieroglyphs, Arabic, French, Greek, Hebrew, Latin, and Turkish.)

Today in Cairo's squares and gardens there are forty-seven statues, including some duplicates. Of these, twenty-six represent Egyptian individuals, but there are also nine busts and one statue of Latin American liberators, one bust of the fourteenth-century Tunisian scholar Ibn Khaldun, four monumental lions, and the granite sculpture of *Egypt's Awakening*. Taking into account the history of each, the overriding themes the statues celebrate are independence and nationalism, and excellence in the humanities.

The upkeep of the squares and gardens falls within the duties of the Ministry of Agriculture and two departments of the Cairo Governorate (Beautification and Cleaning, and Special Gardens). The Ministry of Agriculture maintains the Zoological Garden, the Orman Botanical Garden, and the Aquarium Garden. The Department of Beautification and Cleaning takes on the task of keeping the streets, green areas, and squares clean, green, and protected. The Department of Special Gardens takes care of gardens with a historical or cultural theme that promotes heritage, such as the Andalusia Garden on Gezira Island or the International Garden in Nasr City.

Cairo's earliest statue, the equestrian figure of Ibrahim Pasha, was unveiled at Opera Square in 1872, followed shortly by the standing figures of Soliman Pasha in 1874 and Laz Oghli Pasha in 1875. The most recent additions to the scene (all erected between 2002 and 2003) are the statues of Sheikh Omar Makram in Tahrir Square, General Abd al-Moneim Riyad in his eponymous square behind the Egyptian Antiquities Museum, Taha Hussein in Giza, Ahmad Shawqi in Dokki, Naguib Mahfouz in Mohandiseen, Umm Kulthum in Zamalek, and Muhammad Abd al-Wahab on Bab al-Sha'riya Square.

Nineteen of Cairo's statues belong to the three eventful eras of modern Egypt— the reign of Muhammad Ali and the

41

modernization of Egypt, 1805–82; the nationalist movement toward independence from Britain, 1882–1952; and the political and revolutionary reforms that ended British occupation and took Egypt into a new era as an independent republic, 1952–70. The statues wear the clothes and bear the symbols of their lives and times: the sword at the side of Ibrahim Pasha, Soliman Pasha, and Simón Bolívar denotes military valor and high rank, while the statues of the early twentieth century such as Saad Zaghloul, Mustafa Kamil, and Ahmad Maher all wear suit and vest as well as the ever-present tarboosh or fez worn by men of social standing during the Ottoman Empire. Fathi Mahmoud, the sculptor of the heroic statue at Cairo University, portrays rioting students of the early 1950s in western clothes (notably, the women are not veiled), and the later, post-revolutionary statues of Ahmad Shawqi, Muhammad Abd al-Wahab, and Naguib Mahfouz are dressed in western clothes, with no tarboosh.

Public commemorative statues and heroic sculptures remind us all of Egypt's journey from cultural imperialism to nationalism. Over the last two hundred years Egypt has progressed from the Muhammad Ali dynasty through British occupation and on to independence. These years saw men and women struggle to form a national identity. As we scan the names and dates of the statues, pivotal events emerge that shaped Egypt's destiny, nationally and internationally.

Cairo is ... a *Midan*

Cairo is a city where a *midan*—a square—holds history. Within a seven-kilometer radius of the downtown hub that is Midan al-Tahrir, motorists maneuver around squares that are home to a variety of statues of men and one woman. The statues stand like signposts gathering two centuries of cultural and political history around their feet. Their stories may inspire us, but as our days become more hectic, and traffic more arduous, the statues just blend into the landscape: we drive, ride, or walk, horns blare and traffic weaves in furious motion and, suddenly surprised, we notice a statue or piece of public art and swear it must be new, when in fact it has been there for years. The leisurely appreciation of historical landmarks is rarely possible—especially in this ancient city, where monuments date back five thousand years.

Midan al-Tahrir—Liberation Square—functions as an intersection and garden where seven major streets converge to route traffic in and out of the busy downtown area—*wust al-balad*. A bench in the garden surrounding the statue of Sheikh Omar Makram on Midan al-Tahrir is a good spot to reflect on the changes in the urban landscape over the last two hundred years. Behind the statue, the modern mosque of Omar Makram (built to replace an earlier, small, yellow-and-brown striped mosque) hides from view the statue of General Simón Bolívar and his own *midan*. Below is an underground parking garage, completely full each day. To the right the Mugamma' (the 'Collective') is a collection of offices constructed to centralize government agencies. Built in 1951, its design described by its architect Kamal Ismail as "a simplified form of the Islamic style," its massive bulk that dominates the *midan* has come to be seen as an icon of the socialist government of Gamal Abd al-Nasser. To the right is the American University in Cairo, which opened its doors in 1919 to 142 students; today there are some four thousand, who contribute to Midan al-Tahrir's traffic congestion. Fast food eateries, cafés, luggage and stationery stores, and sidewalk vendors underscore the immediacy of the day.

Tahrir Street leads to the district of Bab al-Luq and Abdin Palace, Khedive Ismail's official residence, built in the nineteenth century to replace the traditional seat of the ruler at the Citadel. Talaat Harb Street, formerly Soliman Pasha Street, leads to Midan Talaat Harb, Midan Mustafa Kamil, Midan al-Opera, and the historic district of Azbakiya. Away to the left from our bench, behind the Egyptian Antiquities Museum, the statue of General Abd al-Moneim Riyad stands among the intersecting streets and bridges of the *midan* named for him. To the left of the museum are the Nile Hilton Hotel and the Arab League Headquarters, and finally the renovated Foreign Ministry, the old palace of Prince Kamal

al-Din Husayn. Metro signs and descending stairs on all corners of the *midan* lead to Sadat Station, an underground intersection where millions of people cross paths every day. A queue of new yellow taxicabs forms a line in front of our lookout.

The landscape of Midan al-Tahrir has evolved, and layers of the past lie under the present like a slide show. In 1805, as Muhammad Ali declares himself viceroy of Egypt, the scene is one of sandbars and marshes. Then the land is drained, filled, and planted. The orchards of the 1820s give way to palaces—the first to be built along the Nile banks is Ibrahim Pasha's spacious but humble Qasr al-Ali. In 1858 Said Pasha brings the Italian architects Pantanelli and Piattoli to build his grand palace, Qasr al-Nil, overlooking the island of Gezira, and Qasr al-Dubara. Ismail Pasha pushes through his new urbanization plan, naming the district Ismailiya. He builds his palace, Qasr al-Ismailiya, and the remaining gardens are handed to the government to carve out Midan al-Ismailiya. It is 1869: the khedive connects Gezira to the east bank by an iron pedestrian bridge, the Khedive Ismail Bridge. The straight Khedive Ismail Street connects the bridge and Qasr al-Nil, now an army barracks, to Midan al-Ismailiya, continuing on to Bab al-Luq and Abdin Palace. The khedive builds a small palace for his Minister of Education, Ahmad Khairy Pasha (subsequently owned by Nestor Gianaclis

43

Midan al-Tahrir in the 1960s

Midan al-Tahrir today, with (left to right) the Mugamma', the Omar Makram Mosque
(with the Semiramis Hotel behind it), the Foreign Ministry (palace of Prince Kamal al-Din

and converted into a cigarette factory) nearby. From these palaces, Soliman Pasha Street leads to Midan Soliman Pasha and northward to Azbakiya.

By 1900 Qasr al-Dubara is gone, but the district retains the name (until 1979 when the statue of Simón Bolívar is erected). The success of Ismail Pasha's urbanization scheme is evident in the European-style, multi-story buildings, villas, and new palaces that fill the land around Midan al-Ismailiya. Qasr Kamal al-Din, designed by Italian architect Antonio Lasciac, rises adjacent to Qasr al-Nil. Next appears the neoclassical, purpose-built Egyptian Antiquities Museum, designed by the Frenchman Marcel Dourgnon and

built by the Italians Giuseppe Garozzo and Francesco Zaffarani. By the First World War the British army is at home in the Qasr al-Nil barracks, utilizing it as their military head-quarters, complete with a railway line to Bab al-Hadid (now Midan Ramsis). The Ottoman high commissioner, Ghazi Mukhtar Pasha, resides at Qasr al-Ismailiya and the British build an official government residence where Qasr al-Dubara once stood. Charles Watson, an American, buys the cigarette factory and founds the American University in Cairo. King Farouk erects red granite pillars in the center of the square for a statue of his grand-father, Khedive Ismail. The Arab League Headquarters, designed by Mahmoud Riad,

45

Husayn), the Cairo Tower, the statue of Omar Makram, the Arab League, the Nile Hilton, and the Egyptian Antiquities Museum (with the Ramses Hilton behind it)

and the Nile Hilton replace the Qasr al-Nil barracks, demolished in 1947. The Mugamma' rises over the square in 1951. In 1952 crowds pour into Midan al-Ismailiya to celebrate the Revolution, and soon President Gamal Abd al-Nasser renames the square Midan al-Tahrir and Midan Soliman Pasha becomes Midan Talaat Harb. In the 1970s the colossal granite pillars still await a statue, and a circular pedestrian bridge rings the *midan*: people walk in safety several meters above the snarling traffic. By 1986 the pedestal and the elevated walkway have both been removed to make way for the underground Metro station.

Midan al-Tahrir beats to the daily pulse of the city. It is an economic and government center, a draw to tourists, a residential area for many, and a space for public expression. But the changes will continue as the city's needs roll on. The American University in Cairo will move most of its operations to its new campus in New Cairo; the government agencies will vacate the

The second Cairo railway station, completed in 1893 by the British architect Edwin Bans

The colossal statue of Ramesses II in front of the railway station on Ramsis Square

Mugamma', and the Egyptian Antiquities Museum will relocate to the Giza Plateau. And people will re-invent Midan al-Tahrir with their dreams and imagination.

Meanwhile, in another part of town . . . Said Pasha, viceroy of Egypt from 1854 to 1863, opened Cairo's first railway station in 1856 at Bab al-Hadid. Today this noisy and polluted district, with more than two million people passing through daily, gives no hint that it was once where Amr ibn al-As ousted a Byzantine army and the Fatimid navy docked its fleet. But this place was always a transit point for both goods and people. When Amr ibn al-As fought the Byzantines here it was already the ancient Roman river port of Tendunyas. Three

hundred years later the Fatimids reinvigorated the port for their military use, naming it al-Maks, meaning 'custom house.' In 1171, when Salah al-Din extended the Fatimid city walls westward to al-Maks, the port was already partly silted up and in decline, due to the westward retreat of the Nile. Bab al-Bahr ('the River Gate') was the first gate at al-Maks, and east of it was Bab al-Hadid ('the Iron Gate'), demolished in 1847 by Muhammad Ali.

Travelers arriving at Bab al-Hadid would find luxury accommodations at the Shepheard's Hotel or Continental Hotel nearby in Azbakiya. After Said Pasha's railway station burned to the ground in 1882, the present station was built between

Opposite: Preparations to move Ramesses II to Giza, July 2006

Ramsis Square after the removal of Ramesses II

1891 and 1893 in neo-Islamic style by British architect Edwin Bans.

As Egypt struggled for independence, Mahmoud Mukhtar's monumental sculpture *Egypt's Awakening* was chosen to convey Egyptian nationalism and identity: it was unveiled in 1928 in front of the railway station. After the 1952 Revolution Gamal Abd al-Nasser had Mukhtar's work moved to the intersection in front of the Giza Zoo, at the head of the avenue leading to Cairo University. He chose to replace it with the colossal statue of Ramesses II, the great Egyptian pharaoh of the nineteenth dynasty (1279–1213 BC), linking the roots of revolution to the magnitude of ancient Egypt: in February 1954, the colossal statue traveled from Mit Rahina to Bab al-Hadid. At the same time, Nasser resolved to Egyptianize the names of public streets and squares: the street leading to Bab al-Hadid, Queen Nazli Avenue (named after the wife of King Fuad) became Ramsis Street, and the Bab al-Hadid Square became Midan Ramsis.

The statue of Ramesses II remained on Midan Ramsis until July 2006, when the Supreme Council of Antiquities moved it to the site of the new Grand Egyptian Museum on the Giza Plateau, leaving Bab al-Hadid eerily bare.

Muhammad Ali and Modernization, 1805–82

IN 1800 CAIRO WAS STILL CONSIDERED a medieval city by European travelers. Napoleon's engineers produced plans and diagrams that showed Cairo almost unchanged since the sixteenth century under the Ottoman Empire. The axis of the city ran from Husayniya in the north to Sayyida Zaynab in the south. At this time, the city wall had seventy-one gates, including twelve major ones. Around the city there were gardens, orchards, and twelve lakes, the largest of which were Birkat al-Azbakiya and Birkat al-Fil.

Muhammad Ali began his quest to modernize Egypt when he took over as governor-general in 1805. His rise to absolute power was consolidated by defeating Mamluk uprisings and eventually authoring a massacre of 480 Mamluk leaders and their followers at a ceremony in the Citadel in 1811. He then turned his attention to controlling the Muslim leaders and scholars, the ulema, who supervised property and economic activities in their areas. He began the curtailment of their power by targeting the highly respected and influential Sheikh Omar Makram.

Sheikh Omar Makram, a descendent of the Prophet, was born in Asyut in Upper Egypt and educated at al-Azhar University. He fought for Egypt's independence first from the Ottoman Empire and then against Napoleon's invading army. He initially supported Muhammad Ali and thwarted conspiracies to remove him as *wali* (governor) by bringing many Egyptian notables to the ruler's side. However, after

Muhammad Ali Pasha at the Citadel

Muhammad Ali provoked the sheikh over taxing religious endowment property *(waqf)*, Omar Makram led the ulema into opposition against the *wali*, and was exiled to Damietta. Upon an appeal four years later he returned to Cairo, but was accused once more of instigating a rebellion and was again sent into exile, this time at Tanta, where he died.

Muhammad Ali's challenge in reforming Egypt was to define modernity and articulate how institutional structures could convey the criteria of change—whether discarding, transforming, or building on current ideologies. He brought law and stability to Egypt after years of unrest by eliminating competition from the Mamluks and Egyptian notables. In 1807 Muhammad Ali installed his son, Ibrahim, as governor of Cairo. As the rivalry among Mamluks, Ottomans, Albanian militias, and Egyptian notables was widespread, Muhammad Ali needed loyal people who spoke Turkish. He brought his relatives and compatriots from Albania, placing them in important civil and military positions. This set a precedent of moving family members into official positions, a practice that had been unacceptable under the Mamluks. One individual who gained Muhammad Ali's

Sheikh Omar Makram

Sheikh **Omar Makram** (1755–1822) was *naqib al-ashraf,* head of the descendants of the Prophet, and an influential leader of the community in Egypt at the time of Muhammad Ali's rise to power. He was twice exiled for his leading role in uprisings against the pasha.

His statue was erected in 2002 on Midan al-Tahrir, in front of the mosque that bears his name. The sculptor, Faruq Ibrahim, presents us with a pious man: his right hand, like the minaret behind him, points to heaven, and his left arm clasps a book, perhaps the *Quran*, tightly to his chest, giving the impression that the sheikh was a great teacher. His turban indicates that he was a *sharif*, a descendant of the Prophet.

Sheikh Omar Makram by Faruq Ibrahim, on Midan al-Tahrir

Muhammad **Laz Oghli** Pasha, from the region of Laz on the Turkish–Georgian border, received the trust of Muhammad Ali Pasha and served as his *katkhuda,* or deputy viceroy. This title gave Laz Oghli the authority to investigate the dealings of other officials, and to govern civil affairs. When Muhammad Ali went on a military campaign to Arabia, Laz Oghli foiled a coup d'état by unraveling an Istanbul-sponsored plot by Latif Pasha. He had the traitor killed and destroyed his militia. Laz Oghli was Muhammad Ali's trusted deputy, and also served as his Director of the War Department, after helping to establish a military school in Aswan.

His statue, sculpted by the famous Henri Alfred Jacquemart, was commissioned by Ismail Pasha around 1874, years after Muhammad Laz Oghli's death. Jacquemart's problem was that no one knew what Laz Oghli looked like. Fayza Hassan tells us the story: "Members of the government entrusted with solving this problem appealed to the prominent Sabet and Daramalli pashas, whose families had been close to that of Laz Oghli. . . . While the two pashas were sipping hot tea in their favorite café in Khan al-Khalili, Daramalli pointed to a *saqqa* [water bearer] walking by, half bent under his goatskin container. 'Doesn't he look exactly like Laz Oghli?' he exclaimed. Sabet Pasha took a longer look at the *saqqa.* 'The spitting image of the *katkhuda.*'"* The *saqqa* was taken up, dressed in suitable Ottoman attire, and made to model for Jacquemart. The resulting statue appropriately stands near the Maglis al-Shaab, the Egyptian parliament, in honor of Laz Oghli's duties as *katkhuda.*

Muhammad Laz Oghli Pasha by Alfred Jacquemart

---

* Fayza Hassan, "Once, They Were Kings."

confidence was Muhammad Laz Oghli, who, if not a relative, was from Albania, and who arrived in Egypt after the defeat of Napoleon's army. When Istanbul confirmed Muhammad Ali as governor of Egypt, Muhammad Laz Oghli took the title of *katkhuda*, or deputy viceroy. His allegiance proved invaluable, as he protected the new ruler from a conspiracy to overthrow the fledgling regime.

The antiquated Mamluk military system of recruiting soldier-slaves from other countries proved unsatisfactory for Muhammad Ali's desire to create a modern military force: soldiers often did not speak the same language, and their loyalties were to their commanding officers rather than to the ruler or the country. So the pasha created a conscript army of Egyptians under a centralized command. In 1816 Joseph Anthelme Sève made his way to Egypt via Persia after serving in Napoleon's navy at the Battle of Trafalgar. An incident of insubordination had resulted in him leaving the navy, after which he served in other regiments in Russia, Germany, and France. He arrived in Egypt having conferred the title of colonel on himself, and soon gained Muhammad Ali's confidence. His first assignment was to train three hundred unruly recruits in Aswan, which led to the foundation of a French-style military academy where Egyptians were trained to make up the new army, the *Nizam Gadid*. Ibrahim Pasha, Muhammad Ali's son and the commanding military officer, became a recruit under the instruction of the Frenchman to set an example for his troops.

After a successful campaign in Arabia against the Wahhabis, Colonel Sève employed modern military techniques when fighting against the Greeks in the Morean campaign and against the Ottomans in Syria and southern Turkey, where he helped Ibrahim Pasha defeat the Ottomans at the Battle of Nezib in 1839. Sève converted to Islam and changed his name to Soliman, becoming known as Soliman Pasha al-Faransawi ('the Frenchman'). Muhammad Ali said of him: "There are three men in particular who have rendered me great services. They are Soliman Pasha, Cerisy Bey, and Clot Bey. These are the first Frenchmen that I have known and they have always merited the highest opinion that I have of them and of France."[13] In 1844 a military school connected to the Egyptian consulate opened in Paris, with a curriculum specializing in military science. Soliman Pasha selected the first class to attend the school, which included two of Ibrahim Pasha's sons, Ismail and Ahmed.

Soliman Pasha married Maryam, a daughter of Muhammad Ali, and spent his remaining years in Cairo, where he died in 1860. His daughter Nazli Hanem married Ismail Pasha's prime minister, and his granddaughter Nazli Sabri was the wife of King Fuad and the mother of King Farouk. Soliman Pasha is buried with his wife in Old Cairo.

55

Opposite:
Soliman Pasha
al-Faransawi stands
proudly behind
Ibrahim Pasha at
the Citadel

Henri Alfred Jacquemart's statue of **Soliman Pasha** al-Faransawi (1788–1860), formerly Colonel Joseph Anthelme Sève, portrays him in the uniform of the French Zouave infantry, recalling his dual nationality. Born French, a convert to Islam, he lived a soldier's life in France, serving under Bonaparte, but rose to prominence as Muhammad Ali's military chief-of-staff.

A detail of Jacquemart's work on Soliman Pasha

Ismail Pasha, the grandson of Muhammad Ali, commissioned Jacquemart to sculpt Soliman Pasha. As Ismail Pasha carried on his grandfather's mandate of modernization by looking to Europe for the latest in industry and technology, Soliman Pasha personifies Egypt's European quest for cultural diversification and a foothold in the international arena, at the same time demonstrating the acceptance of foreigners who integrate into the Egyptian culture. From 1874 to 1964 Soliman Pasha's statue stood on the downtown square that bore his name, now Talaat Harb Square. The statue faced toward the Azbakiya Gardens and the statue of Ibrahim Pasha, also erected in 1874. In the new revolutionary ethos Soliman Pasha's statue was replaced in 1964 by the modern Egyptian hero Talaat Harb, and moved to its present location at the entrance to the Citadel's Military Museum.

Soliman Pasha's Mausoleum stands near the Corniche in Old Cairo, across from the southern tip of Roda Island. Karl von Dibitsch was the architect of this 1862 mausoleum, which has recently been renovated.

When the Ottoman sultan asked Muhammad Ali to suppress the Wahhabi revolt in Arabia, the Ottoman–Egyptian army was initially led by his young son, Tusun, but after his premature death in 1816 the ruler's eldest son, Ibrahim, took over the military command. Ibrahim Pasha proved to have a superior disposition for strategy, and quickly destroyed the Wahhabis' political power and captured Medina in 1816.

With Arabia now under Ottoman control, Ibrahim Pasha led his army through the hostile desert and conquered the Sudanese territories between 1820 and 1822. Again, the Ottoman sultan requested Muhammad Ali's help, this time to suppress a Greek revolt, and in 1824 Ibrahim Pasha led the Ottoman–Egyptian army of seventeen thousand through Crete, Cyprus, and Morea, eventually capturing Athens in 1826.

Soliman Pasha al-Faransawi, by Alfred Jacquemart

The Konia Victory, by Jules Cordier, bas relief on the pedestal of the statue of Ibrahim Pasha

Opposite: Ibrahim Pasha, by Charles Henri Joseph Cordier

Ibrahim Pasha (1789–1848), born in Kavalla (now in Greece), was Muhammad Ali's eldest son and general of the Ottoman–Egyptian army, governor of Syria, and briefly viceroy of Egypt, a man known for his love of horses, his courage, and, at times, his ruthlessness.

Twenty-five years after his death his son, Khedive Ismail, presided over the unveiling of the equestrian statue at Azbakiya in front of the newly built Opera House. Charles Henri Joseph Cordier, the French sculptor commissioned by Ismail, depicted Ibrahim as a man ready to protect and expand Muhammad Ali's domain with trusted steed and guiding finger. Ismail Pasha, in the midst

of his urbanization and Europeanization of downtown Cairo, had his father's statue erected to remind the populace of the family's dynastic succession and their role as pioneers of modernization.

On either side of the granite base are two bas-relief friezes depicting Ibrahim Pasha defeating the Ottomans at the battles of Acre in May 1832 and Konya in December 1832. When it was first erected Turkish objections led to the removal of these friezes; it was not until a century later that they were reinstated, when the sculptor's grandson, Jules Cordier, recreated the same scenes based on photographs of the marble

Ibrahim Pasha in front of the original Opera House, which burned down in 1971

originals. Two figures in the friezes are worthy of note: the woman standing behind Ibrahim probably represents Egypt; a man dressed in European attire may well be Soliman Pasha al-Faransawi.

During the Orabi revolution of the early 1880s, Colonel Orabi's disapproval of heroic images encouraged a mob to pull down the equestrian statue of Ibrahim Pasha, but it was taken to the Egyptian Museum for safekeeping until the end of the uprising,

when it was reinstalled by Khedive Tawfiq. A replica stands at the entrance to the Citadel's Military Museum.

The Opera House is long gone, burned down in 1971 and now replaced by a modest shopping mall and multistory parking garage. The word on the street is that the statue will follow in the footsteps of Ramesses II and be moved to a museum, but for now Ibrahim Pasha still sits astride his horse, pointing confidently to the future.

Muhammad Ali's vision of expansionism included the control of Syria, and this meant turning on his patron the Ottoman sultan. Ibrahim Pasha directed his troops into Palestine and Syria, conquering Sidon, Beirut, Tripoli, and Damascus, and continuing his march into Anatolia, where he defeated the sultan's army near Konya. Britain and France interceded to divert Ibrahim Pasha from marching toward Istanbul, and negotiations with the Ottoman sultan gave major concessions to

Muhammad Ali, who gained control over Syria and Crete. Now the ruler and his son controlled lands from the Sudan to the Levant, giving Egypt a regional dominance and protecting the country from invasion.

Ibrahim helped his father unite and maintain his authority by supervising all government departments and officials and overseeing the reforms that the ruler initiated. Muhammad Ali's overall determination and vision of a modernized Egypt was to focus on the economy, transportation, education, and opening up of the country internationally, particularly toward Europe. Education was crucial for reforms to be effective. Recognizing this dilemma, Muhammad Ali introduced the first advanced educational institutions to Egypt, such as the Qasr al-Aini Medical School, founded in 1827, and the School of Translation, established in 1830. Men chosen to study in Europe and educated in these new institutions played key roles in development projects that continued throughout the nineteenth century. Educated sons of prosperous landowners, miltary officers, and civil servants became the basis of a professional class of Egyptians; and with the opening of government schools, youth were educated under government-controlled curricula, which provided a more diverse education than the village Quranic schools. As more opportunities were made available for European travel and study, a precedent was set that different ideologies and cultures were worthy of consideration, and an assimilation of western civilization began.

Ibrahim Pasha, deeply committed to his father's modernization policies, supported his directives to maintain the condition of streets, upgrade the appearance of Cairo, and construct major roads. One edict was to drain and fill in the lakes and stabilize the riverbanks in response to growing concerns that the water, stagnant in the dry season, caused disease. Once the ponds were drained, the level of the land was raised to prevent further flooding from the Nile. Meanwhile Ibrahim stabilized the east bank of the river by planting fast-growing figs and orange trees, the basis for pleasure gardens and plantations. André Raymond writes: "A number of public works were undertaken to prepare the way for future developments. The mounds of debris surrounding Cairo were leveled along the north and west borders. And the grading and planning carried out under Ibrahim Pasha of some 160 hectares in the zone between the city and the Nile behind the flood dike facilitated the urban development projects ultimately undertaken by Ismail Pasha."[14] Among his orchards and banyan trees along the Nile Ibrahim Pasha built a palace, Qasr al-Ali, which was later torn down to accommodate the urbanization in the district of Qasr al-Dubara and Garden City. Prince Muhammad Ali Tawfiq preserved part of his great-grandfather's magnificent gardens by building his Manial Palace on Roda Island in 1919.

In 1848 Ibrahim Pasha briefly inherited his father's title of viceroy when Muhammad Ali's health and mental capacity deteriorated, but he died before his father after a long battle with an illness contracted when on an expedition searching for the source of the Nile. His military campaigns had earned him the position of governor in the Levant, where he followed his father's vision and introduced economic reforms, becoming quite popular with the people. If it were not for Ibrahim Pasha's statue standing on Opera Square for nearly 150 years, might we forget this colorful figure in Egyptian history? His father, who ruled Egypt for four decades, and Ibrahim's son, Khedive Ismail, who opened Egypt to Europe, can easily overshadow his memory. Yet the population of southern Turkey remember him for his reform policies, Europeans remember him as a great soldier, and Egyptians remember him as a military strategist and conservationist.

Abbas Hilmi I (r. 1848–54), grandson of Muhammad Ali, took control of Egypt after Ibrahim's death, followed by Said Pasha (r. 1854–63), son of Muhammad Ali. After the death of Said Pasha, Ismail Pasha (r. 1863–79), son of Ibrahim Pasha, ruled Egypt.

Abbas Hilmi I, who succeeded his grandfather Muhammad Ali, built barracks to the northeast of Azbakiya. Though he was not open to foreign intervention like his predecessors, he did sign the contract with the British to build Egypt's railway system, which opened up Cairo to the Mediterranean Sea: in 1856 the first railway station in the Middle East and Africa was inaugurated in Cairo at Bab al-Hadid. Abbas's successor, Said Pasha, built his palace, Qasr al-Nil ('the Nile Palace'), on the river's eastern bank, and continued railway expansion under British contract.

The next ruler, from 1863 to 1879, was Ismail Pasha, granted the title khedive by the Ottoman sultan Abdulhamid. Born in Cairo and educated in Vienna and Paris, Ismail was in the right place at the right time to carry through Muhammad Ali's modernization policies. He had been familiar with the old Paris but Baron Haussmann's extensive urban renewal project changed the face of the French capital after 1853, cutting through the narrow, winding roads to make way for broad boulevards and the incorporation of squares and parks. When Ismail returned to Paris for the Exposition Universelle in 1867 he found a changed city, and its gardens, boulevards, and elegant promenades inspired him to imitate Haussmann's vision in Cairo by creating a new city layout with grids of streets, and boulevards radiating from squares.

In 1863, the population of Cairo was 270,000, living in the area from the Mosque of Amr ibn al-As to the district of Husayniya in the north, but from the Citadel to Azbakiya, most of the quarters were run down and cut off from the Nile by ponds, swamps, tombs, and hills. The khedive put all his efforts into the development of

Azbakiya and a new district between there and the Nile (today's Tahrir and Qasr al-Nil), which he named after himself: Ismailiya. He enlisted engineers, botanists, architects, artisans, and translators from France and Italy. He employed the French-educated Egyptian Ali Mubarak to oversee French engineers and technicians. Reclaimed swampland came under a system devised by the ruler that offered free land to anyone who would construct a European-style building worth thirty thousand francs and within two years. Jean-Pierre Barillet-Deschamps, a highly acclaimed French landscape gardener, was employed to re-model the Azbakiya area, fashioning it after Parc Monceau in Paris. Gaslights illuminated nearly twenty acres of green lawns, botanical gardens, paths, grottos, open-air cafés, and theaters. The garden was enclosed with railings and gates, and from time to time an entrance fee was charged.

But the scheme had its casualties: Ismail ordered Mamluk buildings and palaces to be demolished. Nearly four hundred monuments were destroyed in the wake of Muhammad Ali Street alone. The Azbak Mosque, from which the district of Azbakiya took its name, was taken down. The only monument to survive in the area was the Mosque of Uthman Katkhuda, built in 1734 on what is now the corner of Qasr al-Nil and Gumhuriya Streets. When the khedive inaugurated Muhammad Ali Street (al-Qal'a Street), it extended 2.5 kilometers between Bab al-Hadid (Ramsis Square)

and the Citadel. On both sides, archways covered the sidewalks to protect the pedestrians from sunshine and heat.

Like preceding dynasties, Ismail created two distinct cities: the old Islamic Cairo remained untouched alongside the remodeled Azbakiya and the new Ismailiya. Ordinary Egyptians lived in the old Islamic, Coptic, and Jewish areas, while the new designation of space to the west was regulated for foreigners and wealthy Egyptians who sought a western style of city life, shielding them from the Egyptian milieu. In Ismailiya and Azbakiya men and women intermingled freely in public places, and no one frowned upon the consumption of alcohol or gambling. In 1875 Charles Dudley Warner, an American, stayed at the original Shepheard's Hotel. "We are in the Frank quarter called the Ezbekeëh [Azbakiya], which was many years ago a pond during high water, then a garden with a canal round it, and is now built over with European houses and shops, except the square reserved for the public garden. From the old terrace in front of the hotel, where the traveler used to look on trees, he will see now only raw new houses and a street usually crowded with passersby and rows of sleepy donkeys and their voluble drivers."[15] Azbakiya in its day was the fashionable center of Cairo: the home of the original Opera House, elegant hotels, manicured gardens, European cafés and boutiques, bookstores and galleries, the place where the European community resided,

63

foreign travelers and dignitaries stayed, and the Egyptian élite visited.

In the public squares of Paris and London statues of European generals and noblemen had also caught Ismail's attention, and he added to the new streets and squares of Cairo another innovation: heroic statues in public spaces, starting with his own family. He commissioned the famous French sculptor, Henri Alfred Jacquemart, to cast a lifesize equestrian statue of his grandfather, and Charles Henri Joseph Cordier—whose busts of African and Arab men were highly esteemed in France—to make a statue and bust of himself and an equestrian statue of Ibrahim Pasha. The two equestrian statues debuted on the Champs Elysées in Paris in 1872, before being shipped to Alexandria. Clearly, the message to the Europeans—and Ottomans too—was that Ismail intended to remain as ruler of Egypt, and that he was stepping into his rightful shoes in a chain of succession.

Muhammad Ali's statue was unveiled in 1873 in Alexandria, where it still stands in what is now Midan al-Tahrir. In the same year Ibrahim's statue was erected in Azbakiya, in front of the great Opera House that had opened just a few years earlier. (Initially known as Midan al-Teatro, then Midan Ibrahim Pasha, this square was formally named Midan al-Opera in 1952.) Jacquemart's four bronze lions were to stand guard around Muhammad Ali's statue—but instead they were mounted at each end of the newly built Khedive Ismail Bridge that

linked Ismailiya with Gezira Island. Now Ismail Pasha commissioned Jacquemart to complete two more statues—that of Soliman Pasha, unveiled on Soliman Pasha Square in 1874 (and now at the entrance to the Citadel's Military Museum), and Laz Oghli Pasha, erected in 1875.

While Jacquemart and Cordier successfully gained Khedive Ismail's favor, other sculptors did not. Fréderic Auguste Bartholdi had toured Yemen and Egypt in 1855–56, and upon his return to France received a commission to sculpt a statue of Jean François Champollion, the Egyptologist who had deciphered the hieroglyphs on the Rosetta Stone. The statue was displayed in the Egyptian pavilion at the 1867 Exposition Universelle in Paris. Bartholdi had offered to design a lighthouse in the form of an Egyptian peasant woman to commemorate the opening of the Suez Canal in 1869, but Ismail declined. (Bartholdi's best-known work, the Statue of Liberty, unveiled in New York harbor in 1886, is thought to be a reworking of the Suez Canal lighthouse design.) Bartholdi next presented Ismail with sketches for a monument to be placed where the ruler would be buried; again, however, Ismail was not impressed, and Bartholdi would never see one of his sculptures on Egyptian soil.

One of the three Egyptian pavilions at the Exposition Universelle, awarded more than twenty medals for originality, creativity, culture, and opulence, was a pharaonic temple designed by Auguste Mariette,

The first Qasr al-Nil Bridge, with lions by Alfred Jacquemart

Qasr al-Nil Bridge today

protector of Khedive Ismail's ancient artifacts and founder of the Bulaq Museum for Antiquities in Cairo. Hassan Hassan writes, "At the great Paris Exhibition of 1867, the Egyptian Pavilion aroused international enthusiasm with its magnificent pharaonic treasures, which were exhibited within a reproduction of an ancient temple. The Empress Eugénie did not hesitate to ask the khedive—on behalf of the French government—for the fabulous jewels of queen Ahhotep, and for the rest of the antiquities displayed . . . . But by then the law prohibiting the exportation of antiquities from the country had been passed, and the khedive was able to reply quite firmly: 'Madam, there is someone at Bulaq who wields greater power over these matters than myself.'"[16]

Auguste Mariette was born in Boulogne, France, the child of a civil servant. He distinguished himself in school and through a twist of fate took the position of assistant to Jean François Champollion. While organizing the papers of the man who deciphered the hieroglyphs of the Rosetta Stone, he became passionate about Egyptology. In 1850 he accepted a position with the Louvre Museum to travel to Egypt to purchase Coptic, Syriac, Arabic, and Ethiopic manuscripts. Upon reaching Egypt his interest shifted to the antiquities of Saqqara and, encouraged by the first-century writing of Strabo and the eighteenth-century discovery

Opposite: One of Jacquemart's lions, facing east on Qasr al-Nil Bridge

The plaque on Qasr al-Nil Bridge: "Khedive Ismail Bridge. Founded in the reign of His Majesty King Fuad I. Opened by His Majesty 12 Safar 1352, 6 June 1933"

of the Serapeum by Paul Lucas, he went on to find the sarcophagi of the Apis bulls. He founded the Service for the Conservation of Antiquities, which aimed to prevent the pillage of ancient Egyptian treasures and their export from the country. In 1858 he became the conservator of the khedive's magnificent collection of ancient treasures and moved his family to Cairo. He opened the Bulaq Museum, and explored pyramids, temples, and monuments, providing the world with brilliant discoveries.

The Azbakiya Gardens was the site chosen by Khedive Ismail to build the Opera House, designed by Italian architects Fasciotti and Rossia as a replica of La Scala in Milan. It was the first opera house in Africa or the Middle East, built to celebrate the opening of the Suez Canal in 1869, and Ismail wanted an Egypt-themed opera at its opening. He commissioned Mariette to write the libretto, based on a book he had written, *La Fiancée du Nil*. Mariette persuaded the khedive to commission Giuseppe Verdi to compose the score. But Verdi declared himself too busy to complete anything in time for the opening of the Canal, though he did accept Mariette's libretto, and with it went on to compose one of his greatest operas, *Aida*. In the meantime Verdi's existing opera *Rigoletto* was chosen for the opening of the Opera House and the Suez Canal. *Aida* eventually premiered in Cairo on 24 December 1871, to great acclaim.

Mariette Pasha

Auguste Ferdinand François **Mariette Pasha** (1821–81) was an Egyptologist who was sent to Egypt by the French government. One of his best-known excavations was the Serapeum at Saqqara. He was appointed curator of Khedive Ismail's ancient artifacts and founded the Cairo Museum of Antiquities in its first premises at Bulaq. For his services to the country Ismail conferred on him the title of pasha.

Until the statues of Sheikh Omar Makram and General Abd al-Moneim Riyad were erected in Midan al-Tahrir at the beginning of the twenty-first century, Mariette's was the only statue in the area, albeit behind a high iron fence in the garden of the Egyptian Antiquities Museum. Denys Pierre Puech's statue, completed in 1902, depicts Mariette with confidence and determination. His Biedermeirer frock coat was elegant attire for a European man in the Victorian era, but the tarboosh instead of a top hat references his years of service to Khedive Ismail and Egypt. By all accounts, the portrayal is befitting of Mariette Pasha, who zealously protected all forms of ancient Egyptian antiquities, insisting that the treasures remain in the country. In 1877 he became seriously ill, and he died in Cairo in 1881; his remains are interred in a sarcophagus beside his statue in the garden of the Egyptian Antiquities Museum.

Opposite: Auguste Ferdinand François Mariette Pasha, by Denys Pierre Puech

Nationalism and Independence 1882–1952

BETWEEN 1882 AND 1925 A REORGANIZATION of laws came into effect that regulated building permission and provided services for street maintenance, planting of trees, and streetlights. The government implemented a tax scheme to preserve monuments, widen roads, improve streets in older districts, and provide better sanitation. In 1897 the draining of the Khalig al-Misri made way for a new form of transportation, the tramway. New bridges across the Nile, new roads, and the tramway all boosted mobility, and Cairo began to expand rapidly. Heliopolis, Shubra, Abbasiya, and Qubba saw massive growth, although—except for Heliopolis—little or no thought was given to urban planning.

Heliopolis was a model satellite town carved out of the desert northeast of Cairo by its visionary and promoter, Baron Edouard Empain, a Belgian who had made his wealth in Europe and Africa. Baron Empain came to Cairo to set up Egypt's first tramway and saw the opportunity to develop an area of twenty-five square kilometers of desert with a self-sufficient and modern infrastructure. Between 1907 and 1919 Baron Empain perfected Heliopolis as a zoned development with schools, sport facilities, green spaces, recreational parks and racecourse, residential and commercial area, and an industrial area to provide employment. Unlike Khedive Ismail's vision of a new Paris on the Nile, however, Empain opted for an overall Islamic and oriental architectural style, reflecting the culture of the country.

Freedom and Agriculture by Mahmoud Mukhtar—bronze bas-relief on the Saad Zaghloul monument

Britain occupied Egypt from 1882, and although the occupation officially ended in 1922 the last British troops did not leave the country until 1954. Three entities fought to rule Egypt over these seventy years: the royal family, the British, and the nationalists. Intrigue was rife, as one can well imagine in a triangular relationship; the pull for power stretched and twisted in all directions, always under the rubric of 'for Egypt.'

Khedive Ismail's lavish spending had resulted in crippling debts, leading to Egypt's descent into bankruptcy. He was forced to sell Egypt's shares in the Suez Canal to Britain and France and to hand over to those governments the ministries of finance and public works respectively. In 1879 the Ottoman sultan handed down one final sovereign decree: to remove Khedive Ismail from office and replace him with his son, Tawfiq. With the change in ruler young intellectuals and landowners believed there would be constitutional reform, but this did not happen and there was a military uprising. Tawfiq asked the British to send in forces to quell the revolt, assuming that after restoring order they would leave. But once invited into the country it was in Britain's favor to remain in Egypt to protect its investments in the Suez Canal. The British government dismissed the Egyptian army, leaving only a British military presence in place.

It took almost ten years for the population to realize that the British were not going to leave. When Khedive Tawfiq died in 1892, the sixteen-year-old Abbas Hilmi II succeeded him. He tried to demonstrate his independence, but Lord Cromer, the British Consul-General, threatened him with deposition if he sided with Turkey or did not follow orders. However, Lord Cromer would not find the Egyptians as biddable as in the past. Young intellectuals began to form their nationalistic movement on the platform of 'Egypt for the Egyptians.'

The Syrians continued to serve as clerks and secretaries and took on the major responsibilities of drafting all communication and accounting, even under the British. Coles Pasha, a British official, noted: "I do not know what we should all have done without Syrians and Armenians to interpret for us, and consequently the number of clerks of these nationalities rapidly increased, to the detriment of the true Egyptian. . . . I fancy that most of the letters we Englishmen and Egyptians wrote to each other in French were drafted by Syrian clerks."[17] Lord Cromer had great respect for the non-Egyptians who served the British in an official capacity, but he was also aware of Egyptian resentment toward other nationalities favored by the British. Competition is a good stimulant for growth, as long as circumstances such as education and economics are relatively equal. Egyptians had a great deal of catching up to do, as immigrants from Europe and Syria poured into the country under British occupation. By the beginning of the twentieth century the Egyptian school system had begun to graduate students who could fill government positions. As schools produced more graduates and many studied for advanced degrees in Europe, Egyptians became more confident. An élite class of Egyptian landowners, university graduates, and professionals emerged—the *afandiya*. Their ambition and challenge was to rise to high positions in the military, government, and civil administrations.

Occupation of and immigration to Egypt were the historical norm, but Egyptians had had enough and were ready to voice their dissatisfaction. Nationalism was the cry of the day. The first to experience this backlash were the Syrians. In 1893 Mustafa Kamil, only nineteen years of age, led the first student demonstration. Their attack on the building of *al-Muqattam*, a newspaper owned by Syrians and promoting the British viewpoint, directed their frustration at that part of society closest to them socially, culturally, and professionally. Yet it was to the French that Mustafa Kamil first directed his appeal to intercede with the British and persuade them to leave Egypt.

Mustafa Kamil was the son of an engineer who was educated in a khedivial school, then studied law in France. He epitomized the rising generation of Egyptian intelligentsia who were calling for independence and promoting the idea of *al-watan* ('homeland') and *al-wataniya* ('nationalism'). Recalling Egypt's pharaonic history as the path to nationalism, Kamil stated: "We do not work for ourselves, but our homeland which remains after we depart. What is the significance in the years and days in the life of Egypt, the country that witnessed the birth of all nations, and invented civilization for all humankind?"[18] He knew the importance of the media as a political mouthpiece. During his studies in France he expressed his nationalistic views in the newspaper *La Nouvelle Revue*, and was no doubt affected by the writings of Emile Zola. In 1900 he founded his newspaper *al-Liwa* ('The Banner'), backed by Khedive Abbas, and demanded the British leave Egypt immediately. The first articles in *al-Liwa* called for schools of higher learning, and by 1904 Mustafa Kamil was recommending the establishment of an Egyptian college and calling for donations. Following the Dinshaway incident in 1906 (when the British executed, flogged, or imprisoned fifty-two Egyptian peasants accused of assaulting a group of British officers who were hunting pigeons near their village), there were widespread protests, and the country enthusiastically took up the nationalist movement. This encouraged élite Egyptians to consider seriously the proposal for a university. Mustafa Kamil began to fundraise from prominent individuals, which brought Muhammad Farid, Saad Zaghloul, and Qasim Amin together as the first committee to promote the initiative. The Egyptian University opened its doors in 1908, the year of Mustafa Kamil's death.

لا معنى للحياة مع اليأس
ولا معنى لليأس مع الحياة

مصطفى كامل باشا

The statue of **Mustafa Kamil** (1874–1908), a nationalist hero, was commissioned by the committee members of the National Party and was first erected in 1914 in front of the boys' school he had founded, the Mustafa Kamil Primary School on Mustafa Kamil Street and Maglis al-Shaab Street near Midan Laz Oghli. But in 1940 King Farouk had the statue moved to occupy the roundabout that until then had been known as Suares Square, at the junction of Qasr al-Nil Street and Muhammad Farid Street, known today as Midan Mustafa Kamil. (Formerly the square was named in honor of Raphael Menachem Suares, who with his partner had bought large areas of land in the new Ismailiya district and sold it to developers who constructed buildings in the European style.) Originally the statue was mounted directly on the base; however, when it was moved to the square, the decision was made to heighten the pedestal so that it could be seen from a distance.

Mustafa Kamil before restoration

Opposite: Mustafa Kamil, by Leopold Savine

The French sculptor Leopold Savine spent two years between 1908 and 1910 creating a statue to represent Mustafa Kamil's struggle for independence, working at the Fondeur d'Art in Paris with René Fulda. Savine depicts Kamil with his finger pointing firmly to the land, Egypt, and his eyes to the future. His hand rests on the head of the sphinx, symbolizing the rebirth of Egyptian nationalism rooted in Egypt's pharaonic history. At the base of the pedestal, a youthful peasant woman with a sheer veil, hand to ear, represents Egypt listening for the voice of youth and freedom. Mustafa Kamil was against women removing the veil. The fact that the National Party commissioned such a statue at such a time suggests that an Egyptian national identity was emerging and was something to be celebrated and commemorated.

Muhammad Farid carried on the work of the National Party after his friend's premature death. The tombs of Mustafa Kamil and Muhammad Farid are in the Mustafa Kamil Mausoleum, which is in front of the Citadel and the Sultan Hassan Mosque.

Al-Liwa became the mouthpiece for the National Party, al-Hizb al-Watani, set up in 1907 in opposition to any foreign control on Egyptian soil. Mustafa Kamil and his cofounders believed that Britain had no legal right to be in Egypt and that only Egyptians should hold government positions. Both Mustafa Kamil and Muhammad Farid were staunch supporters of Egypt's independence from the British, and at the same time supported the khedive, maintaining his authority to form the government and constitution.

Mustafa Kamil and Muhammad Farid were born into the Ottoman–Egyptian élite that took root during Muhammad Ali's reign. Their families had resources and social standing; their sons were products of Muhammad Ali's and Ismail's schools, an alternative education to that of the traditional *kuttabs* and al-Azhar's Islamic *madrasa* and university. Muhammad Farid's was a landowning family from Turkey, and he was educated in French schools and studied law. At the time of Farid's birth in 1869 Khedive Ismail was opening the Suez Canal and deeply committed to the Europeanization of Cairo. Within thirty years the political climate had changed radically, and Egyptians were prepared to lead their country. Farid became a leader and a financial supporter of Mustafa Kamil's National Party, and upon the premature death of his friend in 1908 he became its president until 1912. Farid left Egypt in 1912, fleeing persecution by the British

authorities, never to see his homeland again. Upon his death in Berlin in 1919, the Nationalist Party wrote, "If Muhammad Farid has been prevented, in death, from seeing the fulfillment of his dream [the independence of Egypt] he at least was able to see his fellow citizens arise as a single man to demand a settling of accounts with the British, a process that can only be concluded upon our obtaining independence."[19] Six months later, Egyptians began their revolt against the British Protectorate.

Members of the Hizb al-Watani were mostly youth from an emerging class of educated Egyptians. The early members of the Umma or People's Party, by contrast, were mainly wealthy landowners and well-known intelligentsia who were opposed to the National Party platform. The Umma Party wanted independence from Britain but was more willing to work gradually with the khedive and the British to find solutions, whereas the National Party wanted immediate independence with no foreign involvement.

One wealthy landowner in the early twentieth century with ties to the Umma Party was Abd al-Rahim Mustafa al-Demirdash Pasha. The Demirdash family was of Circassian Mamluk ancestry, arriving in Egypt with the name Taymourtash around 1517. Muhammad al-Demirdash al-Mahmudi founded a Sufi order—al-Tariqa al-Demirdashiya—soon after the Ottomans took control of Egypt. The responsibility of continuing the order

Muhammad Farid Pasha, by Mansour Farag

Muhammad Farid Pasha (1869–1919) was a lawyer and a nationalist who fought British occupation through the National Party, and a strong proponent of 'Egypt for the Egyptians.' Muhammad Farid Street intersects Midan Mustafa Kamil in down-town Cairo. By design or coincidence this is appropriate since the two men worked together for Egyptian independence.

For many years the statue of Muhammad Farid, the work of Egyptian sculptor Mansour Farag, stood in the Azbakiya Gardens (much reduced since Farid's lifetime), with his back to the congested Ataba Square and a massive parking garage. However, the statue has now been moved to a new perch at the crossroads of Muhammad Farid Street and Bustan Street, near Abdin Palace. The sculptor employs a western suit with tarboosh to denote the typical dress of the élite and educated men of the time.

Muhammad Farid Pasha at his new home at the junction of Muhammad Farid Street and Bustan Street

In 1928, al-Sayyid Abd al-Rahim Mustafa **al-Demirdash Pasha** (?–1930) donated land that surrounded his home, and money, to build the Demirdash Hospital, which later became the Ain Shams University Hospital. To commemorate his gift Anton Haggar was commissioned to sculpt a bronze bust, which was unveiled in 1929 and still stands in the center of the hospital's front garden, along Ramsis Street. In addition, two marble plaques bearing his name flank the hospital's main gate. Across the street from the bust is the Ahmad Maher Mausoleum.

Demirdash Pasha left his fortune to one of his daughters, Qut al-Qulub, leaving his other daughter Hamada penniless. Until the 1952 Revolution Qut al-Qulub lived in her palace at Qasr al-Dubara, hosting famous European authors and poets at her literary salons—a soirée at Qut's palace was the height of society. She supported Huda Shaarawi's quest for women's rights and removal of the veil, and met with the controversial writer and proponent of Egyptian feminism, Qasim Amin. In 1961 the government under Gamal Abd al-Nasser sequestered the family's wealth and land, allotting them a monthly salary. The palace was torn down around 1965 to make way for a street next to the Semiramis Hotel.

Abd al-Rahim Mustafa
al-Demirdash

passed down from father to son, and Abd al-Rahim assumed the mantle from his father, Mustafa, at the age of twenty-four. The Sufi order was made up of prominent scholars and merchants, which, along with his considerable wealth, gave Abd al-Rahim influence in parliament, where he served, in various positions, for nearly twenty years. In 1928, he donated his property on Queen Nazli Street (now Ramsis Street) and 100,000 Egyptian pounds (a huge amount of money at the time) to build a charity institution, the Demirdash Hospital, now a part of Ain Shams University Hospital. This type of philanthropic donation was considered a religious endowment, a *waqf*, and although people already gave money under the *waqf* system, Demirdash's generosity propelled a wave of prominent Egyptians to follow in his footsteps. Stories passed down by word of mouth tell how the government wished to recognize Demirdash with ceremonies and awards for his generosity but he would have none of it, pointing out that only God would judge him. Nevertheless, on 25 November 1928, officials did gather to celebrate the placement of the foundation stone at the Demirdash Hospital.

The Dinshaway incident and its repercussions continued to reverberate. Ahmad Shawqi, 'Prince of Poets,' and Hafez Ibrahim, 'Poet of the Nile,' both submitted works to the newspapers expressing their outrage over the affair. Ibrahim, a member of the Umma Party, wrote: "Kill well if you withhold pardon. Was it punishment you sought or revenge?"[20] 'Poet of the Nile' was the title popularly conferred on Hafez Ibrahim for his ability to express the feelings of ordinary people, in contrast to his rival Ahmad Shawqi. These two contemporaries came from very different backgrounds: Ibrahim from the military, and Shawqi from the palace. Hafez Ibrahim was born on a houseboat on the Nile near Dayrut in Upper Egypt. After his father died his mother brought him to Cairo where his uncle, Mohamed Niyazi Bey, an engineer in the Department of Public Works, sponsored him. He studied at the Military Academy, graduating in 1891, and served during the Mahdist uprising in Sudan, where he wrote verse for the soldiers in Khartoum. When it was discovered that he had petitioned against Lord Cromer, he and eighteen other officers were court-martialed. Upon returning to Cairo he joined the police force and later became an editor at *al-Ahram* newspaper. Much of his poetry was about Egypt's national identity and the struggle against occupation. His best-known work on this subject is his poetry about the Dinshaway incident, and about the women's demonstration during the 1919 Revolution. Although Ibrahim, like Mustafa Kamil and Talaat Harb, did not object to women to being educated, he did believe that coeducation within an institution began a dangerous trend toward liberalism. Ibrahim begins his poem, *The Ladies Demonstration*:

The fair ladies went out to protest,
And I approached to see them gathering.
Behold! From underneath the black
Of their clothes, their hair is shown free!

Women demonstrated in March 1919 for independence from Britain and for Egyptian nationalism but it was clear there was another struggle brewing—for women's rights.[21]

Ahmad Shawqi's background was very different. His Turkish grandfather came to Egypt in the entourage of Viceroy Muhammad Ali and rose to occupy eminent positions, but by the time Shawqi was born in 1868 his father had already squandered the family fortunes. Shawqi's maternal grandmother cared for him from infancy and sponsored his education. He attended a *kuttab* (Quranic school) in Sayyida Zaynab and moved rapidly through school before studying law in Egypt and France. The khedive sponsored his education and journey to France, where he stayed for four years. On his return to Egypt Shawqi became a member of the khedivial court, taking a position as an emissary for the Egyptian government—and as official poet. He wrote poetry that praised the khedive and glorified his political position and about the royal family, themes that did not capture the attention of ordinary people as did Hafiz Ibrahim's work.

At the onset of the First World War Britain declared Egypt a British Protectorate.

Hafez Ibrahim (1871–1932) was known as the Poet of the Nile, and sometimes the Poet of the People, as his writings were widely revered by ordinary Egyptians. His poetry was often about subjects with which the majority of Egyptians were familiar, such as poverty and the politics of foreign occupation.

The statue of Hafez Ibrahim is hidden behind the branches of a sycomore fig tree, almost at the end of the Hurriya Garden on Gezira Island. The sculptor Faruq Ibrahim depicts Hafez Ibrahim as a learned man, though his attire is that of the Egyptian village, with fez and *gallabiya*. The figure seems at ease, with his legs crossed yet with books on his lap that remind us of his love for literature. The sculptor used fiberglass filling over a metal frame, covered with concrete and painted gray—the materials have not held up well, and are in need of frequent repair.

Hafez Ibrahim is made from fiberglass and concrete

Hafez Ibrahim, by Faruq Ibrahim, in the Hurriya Garden

Ahmad Shawqi Pasha (1868–1932) was a son of a wealthy family and enjoyed the protection of the khedivial court. He studied in France and traveled extensively. He was for many years the official poet of the khedive, and at the pan-Arab celebrations of 1927 received the title *Amir al-Shu'ara*— Prince of Poets.

Remarkably there are five statues of Ahmad Shawqi within five kilometers of his Nile Corniche home in Giza. In 1962 the Italian government unveiled a bronze sculpture of the poet created in 1960 by Egyptian sculptor Gamal Sigini, in the Garden of the Immortals at the Borgese Park, Rome. Three duplicates of this statue stand in various Cairo locations: in the garden of Ahmad Shawqi's home in Dokki, at the intersection of Dokki Street and Abd al-Salam Arif Street across from the Orman Botanical Garden, and at the entrance to the Hurriya Garden. Sigini depicts Shawqi in European attire: suit, bow tie, no fez, with a gown draped over his thighs. The bronze statue takes on a formal yet powerful poise. The rose, the manuscript, and the mask of tragedy allude to his sensitive nature and

Ahmad Shawqi, in the Hurriya Garden, Gezira, with General Abd al-Moneim Riyad behind

A detail of the Ahmad Shawqi statue by Gamal Sigini, of which there are three casts in Cairo: in Giza, Dokki, and Gezira

mastery in poetics. He leans forward with a strong vision toward the future. Paradoxically Sigini counters the formality of the pose by crossing Shawqi's legs at the ankles, which adds a casualness and sensitivity to the statue's demeanor.

Another Egyptian sculptor, Abd al-Hamid Hamdi, takes up the casual posture of the poet in the two other duplicate statues of Shawqi in the Andalusia Garden and in the Opera House grounds. These statues were inspired by a photograph of the poet that can be viewed at his house in Giza. Hamdi portrayed Shawqi lounging in pensive contemplation, withdrawn from the world. If it were not for the informal pose, it would seem that Ahmad Shawqi holds court over the Andalusia Garden. But the placing of the statue is fitting, as a ruminative Shawqi perhaps ponders over his Andalusian poem, "In Exile."

Ahmad Shawqi asked that when he died Hafez Ibrahim would write his epitaph, and the poem Ibrahim wrote is etched in the granite pedestal on the statue in the Andalusia Garden:

He came before his time,
Or, after his time.
He used his imagination to climb
A lightning bolt. And then,
Once he reached the top,
He wielded it.*

Ahmad Shawqi, in the Andalusia Garden

Hafez Ibrahim wrote Ahmad Shawqi's epitaph, etched on the granite pedestal of Shawqi's statue in the Andalusia Garden

---

* Luke Dittrich, "Frozen Heroes."

Khedive Abbas Hilmi II, who had never easily bent to the British will (as had his father Tawfiq), was finally deposed and exiled in 1914. Shawqi's loyalty to the khedive, as well as his outspoken poem criticizing the British occupation, resulted in his own exile to Spain. During this time he wrote patriotic poetry reflecting the pain of exile and yearning for his homeland. His poem "In Exile" reads in Desmond O'Grady's translation:[22]

A bird cries out in the valley. Similar
*   our sadness.*
Should I sigh for your trouble or sorrow
*   for my own?*
What story have you to tell me? That
*   the self-same*
hand broke my heart also clipped your
*   wings?*
Exile has us both fellow-strangers in
*   this place*
where our kind never meet. Separation
*   scarred us—*
you with the shears, me with the barbed
*   arrow.*
Roused by longing, we can't move, our
*   broken wings too weak to fly.*
Child of that valley, nature divides,
affliction unites. You haven't forsaken
your drinking fountain for unquenched
*   thirst.*
Sad memory of countless sorrows.
Dragged your feet, trailing your tail
you seek healing.
Many the healers of the body.
Where the healer of the soul?

When Shawqi returned to Alexandria in 1920 his fellow citizens welcomed him as a hero. In 1927 he was formally named Prince of Poets by his peers. He wrote in Classical Arabic, taking his inspiration from the great Arab poet Abu Nawwas and the Abbasid period. During the time of the British Protectorate poets and writers often drew on traditional Arabic style and language in an effort to evoke the time when the Arabs ruled an empire. Poets like Hafiz Ibrahim and Ahmad Shawqi strove to encourage patriotism and remind Egyptians of their heritage. The renowned Egyptian musicians Muhammad Abd al-Wahab and Umm Kulthum incorporated the poetry of Ahmad Shawqi in their music. Shawqi often used the imagery of pyramids and other pharaonic symbols as he wrote about Egypt's problems and the poverty of the present juxtaposed with the glories of the past. He also wrote many plays; his *Cleopatra* was a popular performance in schools. Although sometimes criticized for his formality, his poetry spans the subjects of humanity—love, death, society, patriotism, and nature.

Khedive Abbas Hilmi II had long been a thorn in the side of the British and now, with the First World War brewing, the British decided it was time to be rid of him, especially as he appeared to them to be pro-Ottoman. In 1914, while on a state visit to Istanbul, he was deposed and his uncle Hussein Kamil, the younger brother of Khedive Tawfiq, was declared sultan of Egypt. The British imposed martial law and declared Egypt a British Protectorate, dissolving local governments. Egyptians were outraged. When Ahmad Shawqi wrote a poem in protest, he was exiled to Spain. There were demonstrations, boycotts, and the nationalist movement grew stronger.

At the end of the war a group of men tried to lead a delegation—*wafd*—to the Paris Peace Conference to press for Egypt's independence, but this was blocked by Britain. The leader of the delegation was Saad Zaghloul, a man from the Egyptian countryside who was destined to lead his country to independence. His early education was in the village *kuttab*, followed by four years at al-Azhar University, where he studied law and French. After graduating, Zaghloul was an editor at *Waqa'i misriya* newspaper, then took a post at the Ministry of the Interior; however, during the 1882 Orabi Revolution he sided with the uprising and lost his governmental post. For ten years, he was a highly successful lawyer, representing Princess Nazli in legal affairs and being appointed as a judge to the Court of Appeal. In 1896 he married Safiya, the daughter of wealthy politician Mustafa Fahmi, which helped position him in politics. After studying law in France, he returned in 1906 and joined the Umma Party to support the khedive, as well as the British—as long as they recognized Egypt's movement toward independence. Lord Cromer, British consul general in Cairo, appointed Zaghloul as Minister of Education. Under his first ministry he made Arabic the official language of instruction in all government schools. The Dinshaway incident, which deeply aggravated the population, may have been a turning point for Zaghloul. He served as Minister of Justice for only two years, after which he became leader of the opposition party in the Legislative Assembly.

With the onset of the First World War, Zaghloul's sympathies to the Egyptian middle class and his ability to rally the masses were seen as a threat to British rule. When after the armistice of 1918 Zaghloul asked the British high commissioner permission for a delegation—*wafd*—to go to the peace conference in Versailles and discuss plans for Egypt's independence, the answer was No, and in 1919, he and his wafdist colleagues were arrested and exiled to Malta. This caused unparalleled outrage on the streets of Egypt, and on 18 March 1919 riots and demonstrations broke out, which the British met with force. The 1919 Revolution was a turning point for the nationalists. Egyptian men and women, regardless of religion, age, or class, stood firmly opposed to British occupation, staging demonstrations, violent riots, and countrywide strikes, with much loss of life. The British relented and allowed the wafd to go to Paris, where they stayed for a year without being able to present their case. Their return to Egypt prompted more demonstrations and they were again exiled, this time to Aden, then the Seychelles and Gibraltar.

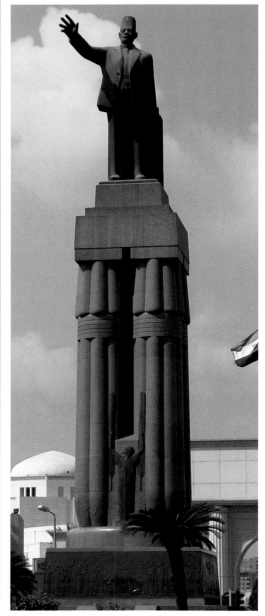

Saad Zaghloul Pasha, by Mahmoud Mukhtar, stands for the Egyptian struggle for independence and liberty

Commanding the skyline sixteen meters above Gezira Island towers the powerful, stern figure of **Saad Zaghloul** Pasha (1859–1927), symbol of Egypt's nationalist movement, his hand raised in a salute to his fellow citizens and the grandeur of Egypt.

Mahmoud Mukhtar, Egypt's famous sculptor and a staunch supporter of Saad Zaghloul, created two bronze statues of the great man—this one in Cairo, and another facing the sea in Alexandria. The style of the magnificent granite pedestal, made by the Italian A. Veccia and designed by Mustafa Fahmi Pasha (no relation to Zaghloul's father-in-law of the same name), reflects Egypt's pharaonic history. Mukhtar's bronze engraving entitled *Freedom and Agriculture*, which encircles the base, illustrates various themes: Saad Zaghloul's individualism, enlighten-ment, women's rights, nationalism, and the rich heritage of Egyptian civilization.

The government commissioned the statue but never paid Mukhtar, who financed the project himself and from public donations and died before it was unveiled on 27 August 1938, simultaneously with its twin in Alexandria.

The statue faces the Qasr al-Nil Bridge (formerly the Khedive Ismail Bridge), the Nile, and the Nile Hilton (on the site of the Qasr al-Nil barracks, which housed the British army). In 1938 the newly renovated Khedive Ismail Bridge was the perfect place for Saad Zaghloul's statue, which stood in front of Alfred Jacquemart's lions, remounted on granite pylons like noble sentinels. With the Hurriya Garden on one side and the

Mahmoud Mukhtar created a visual representation of Egyptian nationalism in his bronze bas-relief, *Freedom and Agriculture,* on the Saad Zaghloul monument

Andalusia Garden on the other, the Opera House at his back and the Nile at his feet, no other statue overlooks such a point in history rooted in occupation, revolution, nationalism, and independence.

In 1928 Mustafa Fahmi also designed the Mausoleum of Saad Zaghloul, in pharaonic style, next to Saad Zaghloul's home in Munira and (now) the Saad Zaghloul underground Metro station.

When Saad Zaghloul finally returned to Egypt in 1923 he formed the Wafd Party, based on a democratic and secular government, with freely elected government officials, and with education and individual rights (including women's rights) as its platform. In 1924 he formed a short-lived Wafdist government. When Saad Zaghloul, the Father of the Nation, died in 1927, tens of thousands of Egyptians poured onto the streets to show their respect for the man who had dedicated his life to liberating Egypt, even though he never saw the Egyptian flag fly over Abdin Palace.

As the nationalists fought for political independence there was at the same time a push to gain economic independence. Talaat Harb, the 'father of Egypt's economic independence,' was at the head of this movement, realizing that without it Egypt would never be truly free of its occupiers.

Midan Soliman Pasha: an older taxi driver might still remember the name, but ask one of the young drivers in the new yellow cabs and they will look perplexed. More than forty years ago the name of this square and street changed with the removal of the statue of Soliman Pasha al-Faransawi, Muhammad Ali's French-born military chief-of-staff. In its place city planners under President Nasser had the statue of **Talaat Harb** Pasha (1867–1941) erected on 12 February 1964, a clear signal from Nasser's government to remove images that would lead the public to recall the Muhammad Ali dynasty.

Fathi Mahmoud, the Egyptian sculptor, assisted by Faruq Ibrahim, sculpted the five-meter bronze statue, which presents Harb with his right foot stepping ahead and a stern gaze looking to Egypt's future. The documents he holds firmly in his hand represent his control of the birth of Egypt's economic consciousness. He wears a formal European suit with vest and tie, and the

Opposite: Talaat Harb Pasha, by Fathi Mahmoud, assisted by Faruq Ibrahim, stands in front of Groppi's on Midan Talaat Harb

In his eponymous midan, Talaat Harb holds documents representing the birth of Egypt's economic consciousness

The Talaat Harb statue by Faruq Ibrahim, in the Hurriya Garden, is made of fiberglass and concrete

In Faruq Ibrahim's statue, Talaat Harb holds the cartouche of Bank Misr

tarboosh that was fashionable for a member of the upper classes.

In contrast, the statue of Talaat Harb by Faruq Ibrahim in the Hurriya Garden in Gezira is made of fiberglass and concrete. In this quiet garden, hidden beneath a grand sycomore fig tree, the sculptor portrayed Talaat Harb more affectionately: the portly figure also wears a suit with a tarboosh, yet he is seated in a grandfatherly manner, proudly holding on his knee a cartouche containing a replica of Bank Misr.

In Cairo in the early part of the twentieth century European languages were spoken as frequently as Arabic, and the downtown stores and hotels rivaled the finest in Europe. During Talaat Harb's lifetime, Midan Soliman Pasha (Talaat Harb probably never considered that, more than twenty years after his death, millions of Egyptians would look up to his own statue in place of the Frenchman's) was the place to be and to be seen, promenading on one of the major avenues, or taking afternoon tea at an elegant café-theater. For those in the upper classes, social life was absorbed with fascinating stories of the royal palaces and political maneuvering. Foreign clubs and downtown cafés were places for gossip and political discussions.

Talaat Harb moved among the small, exclusive circles of politics and business. He was a lawyer and entrepreneur who continually advocated for economic independence for Egypt and the end of the British Protectorate. Before the First World War, recognizing that foreigners controlled nearly 90 percent of Egyptian firms, he encouraged Egyptian landowners to invest in Egyptian industries and established an Egyptian consortium that would use their capital. In 1920, after studying the banking system in Germany, he founded Bank Misr, which backed entrepreneurial projects and businesses ranging from textiles to insurance companies. The shareholders and employees of the bank were all Egyptian, and all transactions and communications were in Arabic. The mission was "to help lift the nation and contribute to the building of the national institutions it needs."

By 1927 the bank's capital had reached £1 million. The Egyptian Company for Cotton Ginning and the Egyptian Transportation and Navigation Company were two of the new companies established by the bank. Airplane travel was beginning to connect the world, and Talaat Harb founded the national carrier Egypt Air in 1932 and promoted tourism by opening the Egyptian Tourist Company. Not to be outdone by Hollywood he also founded Misr Studios, all proving that Egypt was more than just an agricultural nation. By 1959 Bank Misr had £200 million worth of investments. Apart from his visionary and entrepreneurial ventures, Talaat Harb was at the same time a religious conservative; he wrote numerous books on Islamic civilization and opposed the women's liberation campaigns to remove the veil.

As Egyptian society rubbed shoulders with western cultures, prominent writers and poets recorded the changes. Addressing the issues of the day, writers often questioned Egyptian identity. Taha Hussein, for example, wrote: "Is Egypt east or west? Is the Egyptian mind eastern or western in its imagination, perception, comprehension and judgment? More succinctly put, which is easier for an Egyptian mind: to understand a Chinese or Japanese or to understand an Englishman or a Frenchman?"[23]

The doyen of Arabic letters, Taha Hussein was a prolific writer who wrote to bridge the gap between Arabic culture and western thought. His writings expressed the importance of analytical and free thinking, awakening the Arab consciousness by portraying daily struggles against injustices and poverty. They reflected the essence of both Arabic and western culture, never falling prey to an inferiority complex in the face of western literature. Taha Hussein, although blind from childhood, became one of Egypt's most revered literary scholars. Born in Upper Egypt, in al-Minya on the west bank of the Nile, he lost his sight at three years old. His early education began in the village *kuttab*; he memorized the Quran and went on to enter al-Azhar University in Cairo.

At the traffic circle at the main entrance to Cairo University in Giza is a pink granite column fashioned in lotus design. Around the column, scribes representing each academic discipline are etched on granite plaques. The column distinctively recalls Egypt's pharaonic history, as does the heroic statue that can be found inside the university gate off Abd al-Salam Arif Street.

The monumental pink granite carved base and bronze statue combine several styles—pharaonic, classical, art deco. Fathi Mahmoud (1918–82) encapsulates the Egyptianization of a nation, its coming-of-age story from occupation to independence. The massive wings on each side of the six-meter pylon give an impression of a guardian angel, or the phoenix rising from the dust. The two-meter bronze statue of a woman clad in classical robes with a wreath in hand and pharaonic-style diadems strikingly sum up the statue as representing 'Mother

Opposite: The Cairo University monumental statue, representing independence and academic scholarship, by Fathi Mahmoud

One of the bas-reliefs on the Cairo University statue employs the symbolic torch to enlighten the struggle for academic freedom

University'—the first modern university in Egypt. On one bronze bas-relief frieze her wingspan wraps protectively around the men and women she educates. On the other side the frieze depicts those who struggle against occupiers for their rights—weaponless Egyptian students rioting fearlessly against armed British soldiers, reminding us that Cairo University students have frequently been at the head of demonstrations of resistance.

The dome of Cairo University behind the bronze statue

The other bas-relief is a vivid depiction of the Egyptian uprising against British occupation

Arabic language and theology were his particular interests, but he also studied French and began to debate concepts of women's emancipation and ethics with the al-Azhar scholars. Finding the religious environment oppressive, he left al-Azhar in 1908 and entered the Egyptian University on its opening day. Later the university sponsored the continuation of his studies in France, where he delved into the history of ancient civilizations, humanities, and Arabic literature, and in 1919 he received a doctorate from the Sorbonne. Hussein fell in love with France—and with a young woman, Suzanne, who assisted him in learning Latin and Greek, and whom he then married and brought back to Egypt. On his return to Cairo he took up a position at the university teaching history of the ancient east and philosophy of history at the university. Muhammad Rafaat al-Nimr, a Palestinian student of Taha Hussein in the early 1940s, remembers his professor: "You felt he knew everything around him as if he could see. We had the feeling that he was aware of every single thing."

Taha Hussein spent forty years of his life—as undergraduate, as professor, as minister of education—intertwined with the Egyptian University, from its first day of classes as a private university to its evolution into a state university, from nationalism to independence to revolution. The Egyptian University first rented the palace of tobacco magnate Nestor Gianaclis (later to become the home of the American University in Cairo), and in 1908 opened its doors as a private university to a handful of students. Its founders, Mustafa Kamil, Muhammad Farid, Saad Zaghloul, and twenty-three other Egyptians, intended the university to "open its doors to every seeker of knowledge regardless of nationality or religion." As fundraising for the university continued, the khedivial family became deeply committed. The largest gift came from Prince Fuad's sister, Princess Fatima, who contributed jewels worth LE18,000, six hundred feddans of *waqf* land, and six feddans for the campus near her palace in Bulaq al-Dakrur in Giza. In March 1914 Khedive Abbas laid the cornerstone for the new campus. In 1925 Sultan Fuad decreed the university a state university, and within three years it would move to its new campus. The planners chose European architecture in the neo-classical style, distinguishing the university from the Islamic architecture of al-Ahzar University. The broad boulevard leading to the circular, palm-lined drive, the domed auditorium, and the clock tower were at the opposite extreme to the narrow and dense space of medieval Cairo. Only after the death of Fuad did the Egyptian University become Fuad I University and later, after the 1952 Revolution, it was renamed Cairo University.

Over his lifetime Taha Hussein wrote more than fifty books, on subjects as varied as educational theory, philosophy, history, literature, and literary criticism. He translated Greek poetry and described the impact

Greek writing had on Arabic literature and religion. He endured severe criticism from al-Azhar for his views on pre-Islamic poetry, and for his support of women's emancipation and their right to education. He wrote: "It is easy to endure vilification and slander, and I have resolved to bear all such vileness as long as there is hope that in the end we can arrive at the truth."[24] Women's right to education had been enshrined in the 1923 constitution but still needed fighting for, and by the mid-1930s Taha Hussein was able to welcome female students into the Faculty of Arts.

From 1930 to the beginning of the Second World War, industrialization, education, and women's rights were the issues at the forefront of the nationalist movement. In 1938 Taha Hussein published *The Future of Education in Egypt*, in which he advocated a curriculum that reflected social and cultural change and put forth the theory that Egyptian culture was more closely linked to Mediterranean cultures than to Arab or Islamic. In 1941 he became rector of the new Farouk I University in Alexandria, an institution that emphasized studies in Greco–Roman civilization and modern languages and European history (pharaonic and Islamic history studies retained prominence in Cairo).

Taha Hussein and other intellectuals hoped to invigorate Arab culture and literature. Hussein was a classicist and emphasized the importance of integrating modern thought in the social sciences with the

Taha Hussein, by Hassan Kamel, combines pharaonic and futuristic motifs to emphasize his achievements and contributions to Egypt

96

Taha Hussein, the doyen of Arabic letters

Taha Hussein (1889–1973) faces east on the Giza side of the Nile near Cairo University, where he spent forty years as student and professor. The statue is in the center of Midan Galaa, facing Galaa Bridge, the Muqattam Hills, and the sunrise. One might imagine that the positioning of the statue is in recognition of Taha Hussein's early Islamic education—looking eastward toward Mecca—or perhaps it reflects his insistence on looking forward and addressing the controversial issues of his time while always remembering his culture.

Hassan Kamel, the sculptor, won a contest held by the Giza Governorate for his interpretation of Taha Hussein, and the statue was erected in 2002. Kamel presents his subject as almost a superhero, perched high in a futuristic cosmos, gripping a book to his chest, his dark glasses bulging like insect eyes. As he leans slightly forward the flowing Greek robes resemble a cape and create an impression that he is ready for flight. The statue captures the essence of Taha Hussein—not just the man but also his work that intertwined the ancient civilizations with Arabic and western culture. At his Giza villa, Ramatan, a bust by sculptor Faruq Ibrahim stands in the garden entrance.

study of Arabic literature and Islamic history. He re-evaluated Arabic classics by relating the works to Greek literature and came to the conclusion that literary development coincided with social development and cultural traditions. "Our Arabic literary heritage," he said, "is a reformer of our character and a creator of our national distinctiveness, therefore it prevents us from losing our identity."[25] He proposed that Egypt provide free secondary education to all its citizens and promote universal literacy, for embodied in his beliefs was the concept of "knowledge for its own sake," the founding mission of the Egyptian University. Eventually his calls for free education bore fruit under Nasser's government after the Revolution.

Nobel laureate Naguib Mahfouz also endeavored to elucidate questions of identity and nationalism in his writings. In his *Cairo Trilogy* he examines an Egyptian family's growing pains that test traditional values against changing times. We watch individuals grasp at modernity over three generations, from the beginning of the First World War to the Free Officers' Revolution of 1952. In the first volume, *Palace Walk*, a major point of friction develops within the family when Ahmad Abd al-Jawwad's stern authority is no longer enough to prevent his son Fahmy's decision to join a nationalist party or to thwart his son Yasin's political ambitions. The impact of nationalism on the family unit changes the strict patriarchal nucleus, as each son defines and responds to

the call for independence differently to the father. In the third volume, *Sugar Street*, Riyad Qaldas gives his own generalization of Egyptian identity, pertaining to the Wafd Party's secular principles in politics: "All of us Copts are Wafdists. That is because the Wafd Party represents true nationalism. It is not a religious, Turkish-oriented bunch like the National Party. The Wafd is a populist party. It will make Egypt a nation that provides freedom for all Egyptians, without regard to ethnic origin or religious affiliation."[26] In his writings Naguib Mahfouz allows us to live through the metamorphosis of family dynamics as responses to politics, women's rights, and values change over time.

From the age of four Naguib Mahfouz studied at a *kuttab*, and he went on to graduate in philosophy from Fuad I University (now Cairo University). He grew up listening to his father's allegiance to leaders of the nationalist movement—Mustafa Kamil, Muhammad Farid, and Saad Zaghloul. "[27]

When the British occupation began in 1882 Saad Zaghloul was twenty-three years old; Talaat Harb was fifteen; Ahmed Shawqi and Mohammad Farid were both fourteen, Hafez Ibrahim was eleven; Mustafa Kamil was eight; Ahmad Maher was just three; and Taha Hussein and Mahmoud Mukhtar were a few years from being born. With the exception of Taha Hussein, all these men had died before Egypt gained complete independence.

Naguib Mahfouz (1911–2006), author of nearly forty novel-length works and hundreds of short stories, received the Nobel prize for literature in 1988, the first (and so far only) Arab writer to be honored with the award. His statue, by sculptor Sayed Abdou Selim, gives us the impression of an everyday man—a man that we might pass on the street or sit next to in a café. Unlike the formal poses of nationalist figures, the Nobel laureate is portrayed as if walking through the ancient streets of Cairo, and we have a clear vision of a man who is an observer and a storyteller.

The statue was unveiled on 19 June 2003 on Sphinx Square in Mohandiseen, the only one to have been erected on Cairo's streets while its subject was still alive.

Naguib Mahfouz, on Midan Sphinx

Nobel Laureate Naguib Mahfouz, by Sayed Abdou Selim: the large hands emphasize the writer's mastery of his craft

In 1922 the British formally declared Egypt's independence and annulled the Protectorate status; however, this was basically an administrative move as the British maintained a military presence until 1954. Sultan Fuad acquired the new status of king, and a new constitution in 1923 included political parties representing the majority and gave the king full legislative powers to appoint a prime minister, cabinet, and two-fifths of the parliament, as well as to dissolve all appointments.

King Fuad invited Saad Zaghloul to form a Wafd government. However, there was competition between the two men for public support: Fuad had been born and raised in Turkey after his father Khedive Ismail's departure from Egypt; he did not speak fluent Arabic and so was not considered truly Egyptian. Saad Zaghloul was closer to the public and more able to bring the people's grievances into the open. In 1924 Zaghloul and the Wafd Party won a landslide victory, and Saad Zaghloul became prime minister—an Egyptian peasant who had fought his way to the highest elected government position. The relationship between Fuad and Zaghloul was tense. Fuad was an autocrat; Saad Zaghloul the man of the people. Each approached the principles of governance differently: the king interpreted the constitution as giving his office supreme governing rights; Saad Zaghloul believed that the constitution represented the rights of the people, and that he was to represent the majority.

The statue of **Ahmad Maher** Pasha (1885–1945) by Muhammad Hilmi Youssef (Hilmi Taher) stands on Tahrir Street in Gezira, facing west—oddly not on the square and street that carry his name. It was erected with no fanfare in 1950—it was reported that a cloth covering the statue blew off before a ceremonial unveiling took place, so none was held. The bronze statue depicts a short, pudgy man, in European suit and tarboosh, and gives us the impression of a determined leader, his right arm energetically raised forward and his left hand gripping documents. Facing the west and to the right of the statue is an entrance to the Opera House.

Ahmad Maher Square is in front of the Museum of Islamic Art. The street of his name runs from there to Bab Zuwayla, one of the gates of the medieval city, and remains a neighborhood of family-run shops and small factories dealing in fertilizers, barbecue grills, bird cages and wire baskets, butcher's blocks and wooden stools, marble and alabaster products, herbs, coffee beans, *fiteer* and *kunafa*, and Ramadan lanterns. Shops and trades cluster together here as in the Middle Ages. The mausoleum of Ahmed Maher is on Ramsis Street, across from the Demirdash Hospital.

Ahmad Maher Pasha, by Muhammad Hilmi Youssef

Nahdat Misr—*Egypt's Awakening*

No other modern sculpture has received such acclaim as Mahmoud Mukhtar's iconic beacon of Egyptian nationalism and the spirit of the 1919 Revolution. **Egypt's Awakening** was the first granite statue to be erected since pharaonic times, and it was the first of the modern statues of Cairo to symbolize a concept rather than portray an individual. The Sphinx and the peasant woman both represent Egypt. The peasant woman pulls back her veil to uncover her face, signifying Egypt's awakening or rebirth, while the Sphinx, opening its eyes and raising itself on its front paws, reminds us of the greatness of the ancient civilization from which Egypt has been built once more coming to life.

When the sculpture was first unveiled in 1928 it stood in front of the train station at Bab al-Hadid. In those days trains were the modern mode of transportation that led to the future. At the same time *Egypt's Awakening* provided the first impression of Cairo for travelers arriving in the city and their last memory as the train pulled away.* Today, after being transferred to its present position between the Orman Botanical Garden and the Zoological Garden in 1955, it is just as prominent. It faces east; the sun rises over the Muqattam Hills and strikes the faces of the monument as if to awaken Egypt every day. And each day thousands of people pass the sculpture—students on their way to Cairo University, families carrying picnics to the zoo or the botanical gardens, and busloads of tourists heading to the Giza pyramids.

Egypt's Awakening,
by Mahmoud Mukhtar

---

* Beth Baron, *Egypt as a Woman*

Zaghloul was intent on securing a treaty with Britain that freed Egypt completely from outside interference, but he failed. To make matters worse a secret arm of the Wafd Party carried out acts of violence in the belief that this would advance Egypt more quickly toward independence. As part of this campaign of violence Sir Lee Stack, the English commander-in-chief of the army, was assassinated, and this brought Ahmad Maher, Mahmud Fahmi Nuqrashi Pasha, and other Wafdists into question. They were acquitted but were unable to re-join the Wafd Party.

Although Saad Zaghloul was not involved in the assassination he knew of the existence of the paramilitary arm of the party, and the British held him accountable. The king dissolved the parliament, and Zaghloul resigned after only eleven months in office.

When King Fuad died in 1936, his teenage son, Farouk, became king—the first of his dynasty to speak Arabic fluently. Farouk began his reign just as the Anglo–Egyptian Treaty legally ended the British occupation, although British troops remained to protect the Suez Canal. One effect of the Treaty was to open schools such as the military academy to the lower classes of society, which until this time had only admitted the élite. This decision would give men such as Gamal Abd al-Nasser, Anwar Sadat, and Abd al-Moneim Riyad an opportunity to become army officers. The Treaty also allowed for Egypt's entry into the League of Nations as an independent country.

The political struggle and intrigues between the king, the national parties, and the British were rife. Mustafa al-Nahhas had led the Wafd Party since the death of Saad Zaghloul and was prime minister on and off from 1928 to 1952. Toward the end of the Second World War Farouk became disgruntled with the Wafd Party and Mustafa al-Nahhas and dismissed them from government, appointing a new prime minister, Ahmad Maher, in October 1944. Maher was concerned with food shortages and inflation, but he was unable to carry out his ambitious program because in February 1945 he was assassinated as he walked out of the parliament building, having just persuaded the government to declare war on the Axis powers. Mahmoud Fahmi Nuqrashi Pasha succeeded Ahmad Maher as prime minister.

Throughout the two world wars Egypt was economically stable, as industry and commerce grew, women were included in public education, and Muslims and Copts united in the common cause for liberation under the Wafd Party banner. With the end of the Second World War and with Europe under reconstruction, the regional problems in Sudan, Palestine, and Lebanon came to a head, and the British presence was particularly unwelcome.

The Wafd Party wanted the union of Egypt and Sudan, with the immediate withdrawal of British troops; the British wanted

Sudan to have self-rule. Egypt went before the United Nations in 1947 to seek recognition of its union with Sudan but failed in its attempt, and Sudan finally gained self-rule in 1956. Zionists claimed Palestine when Britain ended its mandate over the territory in 1948 and Egypt entered Palestine to fight against the Zionist movement, but the war ended disastrously for Egypt and the Arab states. For Egypt the turmoil revealed the lack of leadership in all quarters: the king's authority was completely in British hands; the Wafd Party was unable to capitalize on its promises to the nation; and Britain, a nation exhausted and nearly bankrupt after years of war, was unable to maintain a large body of troops in the region. This was evident to the Egyptians, and crowds took to the streets on a daily basis, making demands on the government; there were student strikes, and riots.

By 1950 the only garrison the British retained in Egypt was on the Suez Canal. On 25 January 1952 young Egyptians attacked the base. British troops retaliated and surrounded a police station in Ismailiya, believing the police were involved in the attacks. They called for them to surrender, but the police had orders from the ministry of defense that surrender was not an option. In the ensuing battle forty Egyptians were killed and seventy seriously wounded. The violence ignited indignation. On Saturday 26 January—Black Saturday—Cairo burned.

Black smoke darkened the sky over the Azbakiya Gardens as the Shepheard's Hotel burned to the ground. Demonstrators marched to Abdin Palace, moving on to Midan al-Opera and Midan Soliman Pasha. The mobs set fire to the Metro Cinema, the Turf Club, Barclay's Bank, and Groppi. They looted and destroyed foreign shops, department stores, airline offices. Cars were set ablaze. By the end of the day the Europeanized city center looked like a war zone.

The end for the British—and for the Muhammad Ali dynasty—was in sight. People heard rumors and read stories in the newspapers about their king, a puppet of the British, who behaved scandalously in his private life. Egyptians had accepted a divided society, a divided city, for too long. Party leaders had run out of ideas; they had no vision to carry the country forward. Time was ripe for a change. On 23 July 1952 a handful of young army officers organized a *coup d'état*, and King Farouk was overthrown and exiled. The Revolutionary Command Council initially installed Farouk's six-month-old son as King Ahmed Fuad I, but then abolished the monarchy in June of the following year, and General Muhammad Naguib became the first president of Egypt. The status of Sudan and the Suez Canal were the major issues to be resolved, and they defeated Naguib, who was soon under house arrest, and by 1954 Gamal Abd al-Nasser had assumed the presidency.

Revolution and Political Reform 1952–70

THE NASSER ERA brought about transformation, a real revolution. Gamal Abd al-Nasser led Egypt at a time when Nehru, Tito, Mao, Kennedy, and De Gaulle led their countries, and the world experienced an ideological tug-of-war. Although 'Nasserism,' at the time, was not identified as a doctrine, it did recognize a movement around charismatic leadership. It was Nasser's death that defined the term, which became synonymous with radical transformation in the country through equality in social rights and justice among classes, through the lessening of the disparity between poor and wealthy, through the promotion of free education and equal opportunity, and through the gathering together of the Arab states in pan-nationalism and unity.

Egypt's new government under the leadership of Gamal Abd al-Nasser strove immediately to expel British troops, the last of whom left the country in 1954, and to nationalize the Suez Canal, done overnight with panache in July 1956, which led to the attack on Egypt by Britain, France, and Israel in October of the same year.

The government eliminated all political parties, including the Wafd Party. The National Bank (founded by Talaat Harb in 1919) and all stockholding companies were nationalized, and confiscation of the property of British, Greeks, Levantines, Jews, and other foreigners began in 1957. In 1960 new economic regulations were introduced, including the first of several agrarian reform laws whereby

Gamal Abd al-Nasser

Gamal Abd al-Nasser

A statue of President **Gamal Abd al-Nasser** (1918–70) was to stand at the center of Midan al-Tahrir, but plans were canceled after Egypt's defeat in the 1967 Arab–Israeli War. In fact, since Khedive Ismail introduced the custom of placing statues of national heroes on public display, no ruler has found a spot at this most public space in Cairo. Ironically a statue of Abd al-Moneim Riyad, the general banished to Jordan for disagreeing with Nasser, stands in one of the busiest squares downtown, while the city's only public tribute to Nasser is a small bust tucked away in a downtown alleyway, Shawarbi Street, next to a Syrian patisserie.

Gamal Abd al-Nasser, in front of the Syrian patisserie.

no one could own more than eighty hectares of land.

The political talk of the day was Pan-Arabism. Nasser's mission was to eradicate colonialism by developing inter-Arab politics and projects. He forged alliances with other Arab countries, in particular Syria and Yemen. This aim of this policy was to create Arab unity, to strengthen Egypt against Israeli invasion, and to support the liberation of Palestine.

The authors of the 1952 Revolution—the Free Officers—were native Egyptians. Many had graduated from the same military academy that had been in existence since Muhammad Ali's reign. Most were from the same class, and were friends: Nasser, Anwar Sadat, Abd al-Hakim Amer, Salah Salem, and Abd al-Moneim Riyad among others.

Abd al-Moneim Riyad's father, Lieutenant Colonel Muhammad Riyad, was an instructor at the Egyptian Military Academy. Abd al-Moneim began life in the Nile Delta city of Tanta, then lived in Gaza among the Palestinian Bedouins for eight years when his father transferred there. Although his mother was completely against her son entering the military academy he finally had his way, and he graduated with high honors in the class of 1938, having specialized in anti-aircraft artillery, a new division. He then studied English at the British Council (eventually he would also learn French, German, and Russian). During the Second World War he was stationed in Alexandria with the air defense unit, and here he caught the attention of his commanding officers through his skills in protecting Alexandria against Nazi air raids. In 1944 he gained a master's degree in military science, and the army sent him to the British Artillery School in Wales.

Whether developing innovative techniques in radar or in advancing rocketry, Riyad never lost sight of the fact that an army must maintain its professionalism. He regarded the Egyptian army as being in a critical state of indiscipline and nepotism, and warned the Egyptian leaders of a probable disastrous defeat if there were to be a war. He threatened to resign, but as he was the only anti-aircraft defense expert in the Egyptian army he was transferred instead to Jordan. During the Six Day War of 1967 he watched from Jordan, unable to change the course of events. Nasser brought Riyad back to Egypt, naming him Armed Forces Chief of Staff on 11 June 1967. He held this position for only two years until his death in a gun battle at the Suez Canal when his company was surprised by artillery fire. True to his character he stayed with his men, commanding them until his last breath.

Under Nasser's leadership the Revolution took on a clear ideology: national liberation and the fight against imperialism in the region. The nationalization of the Suez Canal and the building of the High Dam at Aswan were part of this drive. But Nasser needed more than grand schemes to unite Egyptians behind their government, and he achieved this by making his relationship with the people personal. He governed as if he stood side by side with each Egyptian family, living their joys and sorrows. He used rallies, speeches, newspapers, education, and slogans to mobilize and unite the nation—his slogan, "We are all Nasser," resonated with the masses. He understood the power of radio, the perfect medium for his charismatic personality, and used it to reach the people by encouraging popular singers to sing patriotic songs to lift their spirits, take their mind off their tough economic situation, and raise their support for Pan-Arabism.

Muhammad Abd al-Wahab and Umm Kulthum were the two leading Egyptian singers of the time, both with a deep love for their country. Nasser put their patriotism to the government's service through public appearances, photo opportunities, and concerts. The music and art of both great masters became an integral part of not just Egypt but the entire Arab world. Their music and personae embodied nationalism as well as romanticism.

The most powerful icon of Arab and Egyptian unity was Umm Kulthum. Born in the Delta village of Tamay, Umm Kulthum

Abd al-Moneim Riyad

Faruq Ibrahim's bronze statue of General **Abd al-Moneim Riyad** (1919–69) was unveiled in Abd al-Moneim Riyad Square, behind the Egyptian Antiquities Museum, in July 2002. The statue, standing at the intersection of Ramsis Street and 6 October Bridge, is difficult to inspect due to the heavy traffic, but the location suits the soldier—Egyptians celebrate 6 October as their victory against Israel in 1973 and the beginning of the return of the Sinai Peninsula. The sculptor offers us an insight into the general's personality—the field glasses hint at his expertise in air defense—but the statue perhaps fails to convey the magnitude of his accomplishments and his lifetime dedication to Egypt's military. A replica stands in the Hurriya Garden in Gezira.

General Abd al-Moneim Riyad, by Faruq Ibrahim, dominates his eponymous midan

Opposite: General Abd al-Moneim Riyad in the Hurriya Garden

came from a peasant home—her father was the village sheikh. She attended a *kuttab*, where she memorized the Quran and learned the beauty of the text through interpretation and correct pronunciation. Her first interest in singing came from her father, as she listened to him practice his recitation of the Quran for religious celebrations and weddings. Eventually—dressed as a boy—Umm Kulthum began to perform at these functions alongside her brother and father, and the audience noticed her exceptional talent. People from the cities began to hear about this young girl with a superior, commanding voice. As her reputation grew she was invited to sing in Cairo, where she and her family received the patronage of the middle and élite classes. As she developed her art she reminded people of their heritage, their religion, Egypt, and the Nile.

To Egyptians and Arabs, the voice of Umm Kulthum—known as Kawkab al-Sharq, the Star of the East—and her interpretation of religious and classical poetry

Umm Kulthum

All the statues on the streets of Cairo are of men except one: **Umm Kulthum** (1905–73). She holds an honored position in the history of Egypt's independence and symbolizes patriotism and virtue by dedicating herself to Egypt. Her statue, by Tariq al-Komi, was unveiled on 6 July 2003 on the Corniche in Zamalek, which faces south next to the on-ramp of 15 May Bridge. The back of the statue is to Abou al-Feda Street where her villa once stood; in its place stands the multi-story Umm Kulthum Hotel. There are two replicas of the same statue, one in front of the Umm Kulthum Museum on Roda Island, the other at the Opera House next to the School of Music.

From peasant beginnings to Egyptian national treasure, one voice uniting millions in song, Umm Kulthum was the pink *baladi* (meaning 'local') rose grown in the Egyptian countryside; her strong voice and insistence on perfection combined with the poets' persuasive prose and the skills of musicians to delight her admiring audiences. Abd al-Wahab said of her singing, "She is a fragrant memory that never loses its perfume."

Opposite: Umm Kulthum, by Tariq al-Komi, in Zamalek

inspire a reverence as solemn as that of the Nile that winds its course through the desert of Egypt. Mustafa Mahmoud wrote: "Umm Kulthum is more effective in connecting the Arab world than thousands of airlines, more powerful than thousands of railways or telephone lines. Get in your car on the night of her concert and roam around the Arab countries, and you will easily identify its borders and landmarks. Her voice echoes in every land. She is the most exquisite audio map marking the borders of the Arab world."[28] She unified the Arabic-speaking public. Her perfect grammar and pronunciation of Classical Arabic, her musical interpretation of poetry, and her beckoning voice captivated audiences. And she used her voice to interpret the expressions of human emotions, love for country, and devotion to God that the poets—Ahmad Shawqi, Hafez Ibrahim, Muhammad Abd al-Wahab, Ahmad Rami, Zakariya Ahmad, and Muhammad al-Qasabgi—composed for her.

Umm Kulthum held performances in open-air theaters, at the Opera House, and at the National Theater in Azbakiya. Radio Cairo broadcast her regular monthly concerts: on the first Thursday night of every month, one voice singing *Watani habibi* ('My Nation, My Love') united Egyptians. In 1948 she donated thousands of pounds for war victims after the Israeli–Arab war, and again in 1956 to rehabilitate the city of Port Said. In 1967 she gave concerts in Arab countries and in Paris to raise money for Egypt's military cause. She called on Egyptian women to donate their jewelry to support the building of the Aswan High Dam.

Muhammad Abd al-Wahab (1900–91) became an Egyptian treasure, writing nearly two thousand songs, sung by him as well as by leading Arab and Egyptian singers. Tariq al-Komi is the sculptor of Cairo's two statues of Abd al-Wahab: a bronze figure in the middle-class district of Bab al-Sha'riya, and a fiberglass likeness in the grounds of the Opera House. Both statues portray the man in pensive mood, seated and dressed in a western suit. However, at Bab al-Sha'riya, the area where Abd al-Wahab spent his childhood, the sculptor portrays him with his *'ud*, presenting him as a musician. In contrast, the statue at the Opera House gives no obvious clue as to his profession, reflecting on his later, successful years as a composer.

Muhammad Abd al-Wahab, by Tariq al-Komi at Bab al-Sha'riya

Opposite: Muhammad Abd al-Wahab at the Opera House

Muhammad Abd al-Wahab and Umm Kulthum met in 1920 at the home of Ahmad Shawqi during an open salon. (The 'salon' was a concept introduced into Egyptian élite society from France: a cultural circle of friends invited artists to read poetry and literature, to show paintings, or to sing. At the Ahmad Shawqi Museum in Giza you can visit the music room where famous musicians, poets, and singers met and gave private performances.) Over the years their paths crossed often, though initially they did not collaborate as their musical styles did not appear to be compatible. But during the years of Nasser's administration the president encouraged the two to perform together, which enhanced Abd al-Wahab's popularity with the public. In 1964 the talents of Abd al-Wahab and Umm Kulthum were finally brought together when she sang his composition *Inta 'umri* ('You Are My Life'), one of her best-loved songs.

Muhammad Abd al-Wahab came from a poor family in Bab al-Sha'riya. His father

was a muezzin and a religious teacher who raised his son with a *kuttab* education and wanted him to attend al-Azhar. He rebelled, and without his parent's permission joined a musical troupe in 1917, where he learned to play the *'ud* (the Arab lute). As a teenager he met the poet laureate, Ahmad Shawqi, who recognized his musical talents, and with the consent of his father Shawqi took the budding musician under his wing. During the seven years that he stayed at the Shawqi home, Shawqi wrote lyrics for him to perform and introduced him to the upper classes and to royalty, and he studied traditional oriental music at the Arab Music Institute, now home to the Abd al-Wahab Museum. He drew on western and oriental music to produce innovative compositions that found immediate popularity, and he introduced the public to songs written for and sung by women in films, bringing women into a public arena previously reserved for men.

Between 1950 and 1960 Cairo's population almost doubled, growing from 2.5 million to four million, and by the 1970s it was a city of six million. The city expanded on the west bank of the Nile in Giza, Dokki, Mohandiseen, Agouza, and Imbaba. A new network of highways and bridges linked areas on the east and west banks. Industrial areas were set up in Shubra, Helwan, Imbaba, and Giza, and adjoining satellite towns enabled people to work and live in the same area. Government developers divided large tracts of land into small parcels for low- and middle-income hous-

ing. In 1958 urban developers began carving out a new city to the northeast, Madinat Nasr ('Victory City'), as a "bureaucratic–administrative town, containing all the major ministries, with housing and community facilities for the growing technocratic–civil servant class."[29] In keeping with Nasser's socialist principles, districts were to be self-contained systems in which to live and work, with housing, schools, government offices, and commercial stores.

In 1952 people went into Ismailiya Square to celebrate the new republic, but by 1954 the name of the square had changed to Midan al-Tahrir ('Liberation Square') as the socialist government tried to extinguish all reminders of Muhammad Ali's dynasty and British occupation. The tarboosh became taboo, as did salutations denoting rank—*bey* and *pasha*—since these were symbols of the Ottoman Empire, the monarchy, and the British. The new leaders changed the names of numerous streets and squares to reflect the doctrine of their revolution: the Ismail Garden became Hurriya ('Freedom') Garden; Ingilizi ('English') Bridge became Galaa ('Evacuation') Bridge; Midan Soliman Pasha became Midan Talaat Harb. Today there are probably few who remember that 26 July Street in Zamalek was formerly known as Fuad I Street, renamed to commemorate the nationalization of the Suez Canal. Of course, Prince Farouk Street was changed to al-Geish ('Army') Street. Ibrahim Pasha's statue survived, but not his name, for the street running from Opera Square to

Cairo, looking east over Garden City to the Citadel and the Muqattam Hills

Abdin Palace was changed to Gumhuriya ('Republic') Street. University names did not escape change—Fuad I University (formerly the Egyptian University) became Cairo University, Ibrahim Pasha University became Ain Shams University, and Farouk I University became Alexandria University. Even the rapid expansion of the suburb of Mohandiseen was affected; as each street was laid down, the names—Arab League, Gaza, Jerusalem, Nablus, Syria, Lebanon—responded to Gamal Abd al-Nasser's drive for Arab nationalism.

The evolution of Cairo is rooted in ancient principles—stones, walls, and the ebb and flow of the great Nile waters. Every turn reveals the human story of those who have built Cairo from the sixth century to the present day: occupiers, invaders, adventurers, immigrants, and wanderers. Each has given expression to his sensibilities, his doubts, his prejudices, and his sense of wonder. They built a city from their aspirations, their accomplishments, and, yes, their failures. Their energies overflowed to transform history, art, architecture, and culture, and we marvel at the wealth of their contributions. Daily we connect with them, learn from them, and construct a new city, our civilization. Ultimately the only thing that can limit our civilization is our imagination. The statues on the streets and squares and in the gardens of Cairo tell a dramatic story of historical events that echo along the Nile, through the city, and among architectural, engineering, and landscaping feats. Each moment in time, never to be recreated with the same people in the same place, unites us by one commonality—Cairo, in its continual whirl with time.

Cairo is... a *Kubri*

In Cairo a bridge is not a road to an end but a point at which to stop. A place to take tea or eat a *fuul* sandwich, to play cards, to meet a lover, to catch fish, to celebrate a wedding, or just to breathe in the northern *bahari* breeze. Fresh air is free on every Cairo bridge. For watching the night pass, alone or with friends, the bridge has the best seats in town. And on any festive day the bridges are playgrounds for holidaymakers. The people of Cairo love their bridges.

Cairenes are innovators when it comes to using space—a highway median for a soccer game, any patch of grass for a picnic, and, of course, the sidewalk of a bridge for almost anything. Just after sunset, refreshment carts roll inconspicuously along the sidewalks, and the colorful plastic chairs are lined up. Sweet potato vendors and *tirmis* (lupine seed) sellers jostle for the best space, but it's first come, first serve. A woman sitting cross-legged fans red charcoal to roasts ears of corn for the evening crowds. By midnight cars line the bridges, vying for space to park. On Thursdays and Sundays in particular a rhythmic honking proclaims the advancing nuptials; adorned with flowers and ribbons, the cars swerve to a stop, doors are flung wide open, and the trilling sounds of the *zaghruta* announce the arrival of the bride

118

Food and drink are always available, even on a bridge

and groom. Cameras flash, recording the happiest day above the Nile's fertile waters.

Bridges are drive-up restaurants: roll down a window and a cool breeze lifts the day's heat as you greet the tea man and order a soda. Fishermen pull out folding chairs and chat together, waiting for a lucky catch. Families spread blankets on the sidewalk and settle into the night, shoes off, playing cards or backgammon, or just watching the continuous traffic and pedestrians. The cool north wind, cooled further by the Nile waters, refreshes the mind, and the memory of the day glides past. By three in the morning the plastic chairs are loaded into vans, the food carts are pushed home, and the bridge is empty but for a solitary soldier on guard.

The Nile defines Egypt: without it, life could not thrive. Cairo's strategic existence is due to the Nile. But as with any body of water, the challenge is to control it and to cross it. At first simple ferryboats were the means of getting from bank to bank, but now ten bridges span the Nile in Cairo. The oldest is Kubri Qasr al-Nil, built in 1872. Khedive Ismail appointed the French engineer Maurice Linant de Bellefond to construct a bridge to connect the island of Gezira with the eastern bank of the river, at the point near the Qasr al-Nil Palace that Said Pasha had built in 1858 (where now stands the Nile Hilton Hotel). The narrow toll bridge, named the Khedive Ismail Bridge, was designed for pedestrians, horses, carts,

Roasting sweet potatoes on University Bridge

and carriages. Henri Alfred Jacquemart's four bronze lions were originally intended to stand guard around Muhammad Ali's statue in Alexandria, but the decision was made to mount them on the newly built bridge, two at each end. Ismail attended the inauguration of his bridge in 1872. Following the construction of the Gezira Palace other members of the royal family began to build their palaces on the island, and when the automobile came to Egypt the Cleveland Bridge and Engineering Company was contracted to expand the Khedive Ismail Bridge in 1913. Another twenty years of city growth and the bridge needed further extension. In 1931 King Fuad gave Dorman, Long and Company of Great Britain the contract to reconstruct the

Father and daughter selling *tirmis*

to the west bank, Kubri al-Ingiliz ('English Bridge,' once known as Kubri Badea after the well-known belly-dancer Badea Masabni, now Kubri al-Galaa, 'Evacuation Bridge'); Kubri al-Malik al-Salih connects the east bank with Roda Island, and Kubri Abbas (renamed Kubri al-Giza in 1966) continues that connection to Giza; and Kubri Abu al-Ela joined Bulaq on the east bank to the northern part of Gezira known as Zamalek. Later, Kubri al-Gam'a ('University Bridge') opened another passageway from Roda to Giza, leading to Cairo University. Since then, connecting Cairo's suburbs has been an ongoing project, linking all parts of the metropolis via 26 July Bridge, 15 May Bridge, 6 October Bridge, and Munib Bridge carrying the Ring Road. All of which is good news for Cairenes—more space to fish, drink tea, celebrate weddings . . . .

121

bridge. Jacquemart's lions were temporarily moved to the Zoological Gardens for safekeeping, returning to their original sites in time for the ceremonial reopening in 1933. The bridge's name was changed after the 1952 Revolution to Kubri Qasr al-Nil, after Said Pasha's palace (later used as a harem by Khedive Ismail before becoming the barracks of the occupying British army, finally being demolished in 1955 to make way for the Nile Hilton Hotel).

With the completion of the Aswan Dam in 1902 and the consequent control of the annual flooding the Nile banks were stabilized, and between 1902 and 1912 four more bridges crossed the river: the natural extension of Kubri Qasr al-Nil from Gezira

Enjoying a warm winter afternoon

Opposite: Rush hour on University Bridge

Preparations for Police Day, on
University Bridge

Bridge banisters make good slides

Opposite: Police Day commemorates
the policemen who died fighting the
British at Ismailiya Police Station on
January 25, 1952

The Sculptors

Henri Alfred Jacquemart

Henri Alfred Jacquemart (1824–96) was fortunate enough
to see his works on display in both France and Egypt during
his lifetime. He was born in Paris on 24 February 1824 and
studied painting and sculpture at the Ecole des Beaux Arts.
At the Salon de Paris he received a number of distinctions,
a sign of royal favor as well as public recognition of his talent
and achievement. Jacquemart traveled in Egypt and Turkey,
studying style and mode of expression, though he secured
his reputation as a sculptor in France. In Cairo his four lions
stand guard at the ends of Qasr al-Nil Bridge, his Zouave-
costumed Soliman Pasha al-Faransawi stood first in
Soliman Pasha Square and now stands in the Citadel, and
his statue of Muhammad Laz Oghli Pasha watches over Laz
Oghli Square downtown. In Alexandria his equestrian statue
of Muhammad Ali Pasha graces Midan al-Tahrir.

Alfred Jacquemart's
signature

Opposite: Forward-
stepping Soliman
Pasha al-Faransawi
was second in
command to
Ibrahim Pasha

Mahmoud Mukhtar

Mahmoud Mukhtar (1891–1934) was a staunch supporter of Egypt's quest for independence and admired Saad Zaghloul's role in the awakening of Egypt. Both men were from rural Egypt and both used their intellect and talents to become leaders in the nationalist movement. Mukhtar's imagery conveyed pride in the customs and life of the peasants and landowners. He carved in granite what Zaghloul spoke in words: *Nahdat Misr—Egypt's Awakening*.

Mahmoud Mukhtar grew up in a village near the Nile, molding mud and baking in the sun or in bread ovens the forms of heroes and creatures from folk tales told by the village storyteller. He recalled: "When I was a child, there had been no sculptures and no sculptors in my country for more than seventeen hundred years. The images that appeared among the ruins and sands at the edge of the desert were considered to be accursed and evil idols—no one should come near." He studied at a

126

Mahmoud Mukhtar's *Egypt's Awakening,* at its original location at Cairo railway station

Mahmoud Mukhtar's signature

Anton Haggar

Anton Haggar (1893–1962) was one of the first generation of modern Egyptian sculptors. His favorite material was marble, which he used to carve statues for the Catholic and Greek Orthodox churches in the tombs in Old Cairo. His bronze bust of Sheikh Abd al-Rahim al-Demirdash Pasha is mounted in the garden of the Ain Shams Medical School, on Lufti al-Sayyid Street in Abbasiya.

Gamal Sigini

Gamal Sigini (1917–77) was a well-known Egyptian artist and sculptor whose works in the 1940s and 1950s helped define a generation of modern Egyptian art. His innovative works were seen in a variety of media, from oil paintings to monumental sculptures. His art expressed his national and Arab pride, as in *This Land is Mine* (1955) and *Young Effendi* (1961) in the Museum of Modern Egyptian Art. In 1940 he founded La Palette, a society to serve artists and the art movement.

kuttab, learning to read and write and recite the Quran. He proved himself a worthy student and was able to enter Prince Youssef Kamal's School of Fine Arts where he met Guillaume Laplagne, the French dean of the school and professor of sculpture. Laplagne's influence on Mukhtar was critical, as he recognized Mukhtar's talent and found sponsorship to enable him to continue his studies at the Ecole des Beaux Arts in Paris.

In 1920 Mukhtar submitted a model of *Egypt's Awakening* to the Exposition Universelle in Paris and won the gold medal. The art deco movement and Antoine Bourdelle's sculptures of heroic figures strongly influenced the young artist, whose art combines pharaonic style with art deco lines that romanticize the environment and the people of the Egyptian countryside.

Egypt's Awakening in Giza and the statue of Saad Zaghloul on Gezira Island are the two best known of Mukhtar's works, but the Mukhtar Museum on Gezira Island houses a large number and broader range of examples.

Gamal Sigini's signature

Fathi Mahmoud

Fathi Mahmoud (1918–82), the sculptor of the Talaat Harb statue on Talaat Harb Square and the statue at Cairo University, also made the mural on the outside walls of the Egyptian Chamber of Commerce in Bab al-Luq, the Press Syndicate on Ramsis Street, and the Court House on Galaa Street.

Faruq Ibrahim

Faruq Ibrahim (b. 1937) is the sculptor of several statues in public view in Cairo and Asyut: Abd al-Moneim Riyad downtown and in the Hurriya Garden; Omar Makram on Midan al-Tahrir; Hafez Ibrahim and Talaat Harb in the Hurriya Garden; and Talaat Harb in Asyut; and he assisted Fathi Mahmoud on the downtown statue of Talaat Harb. Two small figures by him, both untitled, are on display in the Museum of Modern Egyptian Art. He works in bronze and stone, and is particularly attentive to the facial expression of his subject. Ibrahim graduated from Cairo's Faculty of Fine Arts in 1962 and took a

Faruq Ibrahim's signature

masters degree in sculpture in 1972, after which he received a scholarship to study sculpture at the Academy of San Fernando in Madrid and remained there as a teacher. Returning to Cairo he held a number of positions at the Faculty of Fine Arts and is now a professor emeritus of that college. He has a long list of local and international awards for his work in sculpture, receiving the top prize at the Cairo Salon for many years in a row and the Order of Merit in Arts in 1983.

Hassan Kamel

A graduate of Cairo's Faculty of Fine Arts, Hassan Kamel (b. 1967) won first prize in the competition for a statue of Taha Hussein, and his winning statue dominates the roundabout in front of the Cairo Sheraton, in Giza. A brass sculpture now in the Museum of Modern Egyptian Art won awards at the National Exhibition held at the Palace of Art in 2001.

Tariq al-Komi

Tariq al-Komi (b. 1962), also a graduate of Cairo's Faculty of Fine Arts, is author of the bronze statue of Umm Kulthum in Zamalek and its replica in colored fiberglass in the Opera House garden, and of both statues of Muhammad Abd al-Wahab: the fiberglass figure at the Opera House and the bronze statue in Bab al-Sha'riya. His marble and granite abstract sculpture *Construction* (1996) is on display at the entrance to the Museum of Modern Egyptian Art.

Umm Kulthum at the Opera House by Tariq al-Komi

How to Clean
a Statue

IN THE SUPREME COUNCIL OF ANTIQUITIES Department of Restoration and Scientific Documentation on Nubar Street near Midan Laz Oghli is a permanent exhibition on the restoration of statues and antiquities, a laboratory to examine and determine the attributes of the monument to be restored, and a library with books and articles about restoration. A close inspection of the exhibit produces more information about the use of particular adhesives and consolidators used in the process. Here are the steps to a successful restoration:

- Assemble and review all information and past data on the statue or antiquity.
- Photograph the statue for 'before and after' documentation.

Restoration in progress on Jacquemart's lions, Qasr al-Nil Bridge

Opposite:
Saad Zaghloul under restoration

- Ensure the material and specific detergent to be used is free of acid and alkali.
- After testing an area, observe if there is salt formation and clean with purified water.
- Statues in public areas are wrapped during restoration so that applied substances are not exposed to pollutants.
- Mechanical cleaning by scalpel, spatula, and blower.
- Analysis of the surface determines the type of chemicals to be applied, if at all.
- Chemical consolidation and cleaning are applied by brush, cotton, and spray.
- Cracks and holes are filled by powder of the same material that the statue is made of, to avoid expansion and shrinkage.
- Coating with a suitable solution after analysis of deterioration factors such as environment, temperature fluctuation, humidity, acid rain, or man-made pollution.

Talaat Harb

Notes

1 J.B. Jackson, "Discovering the Vernacular Landscape."
2 Manal al-Jesri, "The Prince of Poets."
3 Doris Behrens-Abuseif, *Islamic Architecture in Cairo*.
4 *Ibid.*
5 Ibn Jubayr, *The Travels of Ibn Jubayr*.
6 Nasser Rabbat, "A Brief History of Green Spaces in Cairo."
7 Quoted in John Alden Williams, "Urbanization and Monument Construction in Mamluk Cairo."
8 Quoted in Caroline Stone, "Ibn Khaldun and the Rise and Fall of Empires."
9 Janet Abu-Lughod, *Cairo: 1001 Years of the City Victorious*.
10 Nicholas Warner, *The True Description of Cairo*.
11 Quoted in Desmond Stewart, *Great Cairo: Mother of the World*.
12 *The American Cyclopaedia*, "Mamelukes."
13 Reported by A. Vingtrinier, Soliman Pasha's biographer, 1886, and quoted in Adel Sabit, *Seventy Centuries of History*.
14 André Raymond, *Cairo: City of History*.
15 Charles Dudley Warner "My Winter on the Nile, among Mummies and Moslems."
16 Hassan Hassan, *In the House of Muhammad Ali*.
17 Albert Hourani, "The Syrians in Egypt in the Eighteenth and Nineteenth Centuries."
18 Fekri A. Hassan, "The Reawakening of Memory."
19 Quoted in Yunan Labib Rizk, "Al-Ahram: A Diwan of Contemporary Life (289)."
20 Quoted in Beth Baron, *Egypt as a Woman*.
21 *Ibid.*
22 Desmond O'Grady, *Ten Modern Arab Poets*.
23 Mike Diboll, "The Secret History of Lawrence Durrell's *The Alexandria Quartet*."
24 Yunan Rizk, "Spotlight on the Dean."
25 Youhana Kalta, "The Influence of French Culture on Taha Hussein's Literature."
26 Naguib Mahfouz, *Sugar Street*.
27 Gamal al-Ghitani, *The Mahfouz Dialogs*.
28 Quoted by Azza Khattab, "Lady of Song."
29 Omnia al-Shakry, "Cairo as Capital of Socialist Revolution?"

Mariette Pasha's tomb at the Egyptian Antiquities Museum

Bibliography

Abou el-Enein, Youssef. "Egyptian General Abdel-Moneim Riad: The Creation of an Adaptive Military," *Infantry Magazine*. U.S. Army Infantry School and Gale Group, 2004.

Abu-Lughod, Janet. *Cairo: 1001 Years of the City Victorious*. Princeton: Princeton University Press, 1971.

The American Cyclopaedia: A Popular Dictionary of General Knowledge. Ed. George Ripley and Charles A. Dana. New York: D. Appleton and Company, 1858.

Allén, Sture. "The Nobel Prize in Literature. The Work of Mr. Naguib Mahfouz," Nobel Prize Citation. Sweden, 1988.

Baron, Beth. *Egypt as a Woman: Nationalism, Gender, and Politics*. Cairo: The American University in Cairo Press, 2005.

Behrens-Abouseif, Doris. *Islamic Architecture in Cairo: An Introduction*. Cairo: The American University in Cairo Press, 2004.

Danielson, Virginia. *The Voice of Egypt: Umm Kulthum, Arabic Song, and Egyptian Society in the Twentieth Century*. Cairo: The American University in Cairo Press, 1997.

Diboll, Mike. "The Secret History of Lawrence Durrell's *The Alexandria Quartet*: the Mountolive–Hosnani Affair, Britain, and the *Wafd*," Anna Lillios, ed. *Lawrence Durrell and the Greek World*. Selinsgrove: Susquehanna University Press, 2004.

Dittrich, Luke. "Frozen Heroes," *Egypt Today*, November 1997.

Dobrowolska, Agnieszka and Jaroslaw Dobrowolski. *Heliopolis: Rebirth of the City of the Sun*. Cairo: The American University in Cairo Press, 2006.

The Encyclopaedia of Islam. C.E. Bosworth *et al.*, eds. "Muhammad Ali Pasha." Leiden: E.J. Brill, 1993.

el-Gemeiy, Abdel-Moneim. "Educating Egypt," *Al-Ahram Weekly*, 27 October 2005.

al-Ghitani, Gamal. *The Mahfouz Dialogs*. Trans. Humphrey Davies. Cairo: The American University in Cairo Press, 2007.

Hassan, Fayza. "Once, They Were Kings," *Egypt Today*, December 2004.

Hassan, Fekri A. "Memorabilia: Archaeology, Materiality, and the National Identity of Egypt," Lynn Meskal, ed. *Archaeology under Fire:*

Nationalism, Politics, and Heritage in the Eastern Mediterranean and the Middle East. London: Routledge, 1998.

Hassan, Hassan. *In the House of Muhammad Ali: A Family Album, 1805–1952.* Cairo: The American University in Cairo Press, 2000.

Hawwas, Soheir Zaki. *Khedivian Cairo: Identification and Documentation of Urban Architecture in Downtown Cairo.* Cairo: Arab Contractors Press, 2002.

Hopwood, Derek. *Egypt: Politics and Society, 1945–90.* London: Harper Collins Academic, 1982.

Hourani, Albert. "The Syrians in Egypt in the Eighteenth and Nineteenth Centuries," *Colloque internationale sur l'histoire du Caire.* Cairo: Ministry of Culture of the Arab Republic of Egypt, General Egyptian Book Organization, 1969.

———. *Arabic Thought in the Liberal Age, 1798–1939.* Cambridge: Cambridge University, 1985.

Ibn Jubayr. *The Travels of Ibn Jubayr.* Trans. Roland Broadhurst. London: Goodword Books, 2001.

Ibrahim, Abdelbaki Mohamed, ed. "Cairo," "Cairo II," "Cairo III," *Alam al-bina.* Cairo: Center for Planning and Architectural Studies, Institut Français d'Architecture, 6–10/201, 1998.

Jackson, J.B., "Discovering the Vernacular Landscape," Mark Dorrian and Gillian Rose, eds., *Deterritorialisations: Revisioning Landscapes and Politics.* London: Black Dog, 2003.

el-Jesri, Manal. "The Prince of Poets," *Egypt Today,* March 1997.

Kalta, Youhana. "The Influence of French Culture on Taha Hussein's Literature," *Prism,* 2000.

Karnouk, Liliane. *Modern Egyptian Art, 1910–2003.* Cairo: The American University in Cairo Press, 2005.

Khattab, Azza. "Lady of Song," *Egypt Today,* May 2000.

Kreiser, Klaus. "Public Monuments in Turkey and Egypt, 1860–1916," Gülru Necipoglu, ed., *Muqarnas XIV: An Annual on the Visual Culture of the Islamic World.* Leiden: E.J. Brill, 1997.

Mahfouz, Naguib. *Sugar Street.* Trans. William Maynard Hutchins and Angele Boutros Samaan. Cairo: The American University in Cairo Press, 1992.

Marsot, Afaf Lutfi al-Sayyid. *A Short History of Modern Egypt.* Cambridge: Cambridge University Press, 1985.

el-Messiri, Nawal. "A Changing Perception of the Public Garden," Philip Jodidio, ed. *Cairo: Revitalising a Historic Metropolis.* Aga Khan Trust, 2004.

Mostyn, Trevor. *Egypt: Belle Epoque.* London: Tauris Parke Paperbacks, 2006.

O'Grady, Desmond. *Ten Modern Arab Poets.* Dublin: Daedalus, 1992.

Petruccioli, Attilio. "The Arab City: Neither Spontaneous nor Created," *Environmental Design: Journal of the Islamic Environmental Design Research Centre* 1–2, 1997–99.

Philipp, Thomas. *The Syrians in Egypt, 1725–1975.* Stuttgart: Franz Steiner Verlag, 1985.

Pollard, Lisa. *Nurturing the Nation.* Los Angeles: University of California Press, 2005.

Raafat, Samir W. *Cairo, the Glory Years: Who Built What, When, Why, and for Whom.* Alexandria: Harpocrates, 2003.

Rabbat, Nasser O. *The Citadel of Cairo: A New Interpretation of Royal Mamluk Architecture.* Leiden: E.J. Brill, 1995.

———. "A Brief History of Green Spaces in Cairo," Philip Jodidio, ed. *Cairo: Revitalising a Historic Metropolis.* Aga Khan Trust, 2004.

Raymond, André. *Cairo: City of History.* Cairo: The American University in Cairo Press, 2001.

Reid, Donald Malcolm. *Cairo University and the Making of Modern Egypt.* Cambridge: Cambridge University Press, 1990.

Rifaat, M. Pasha. *The Awakening of Modern Egypt.* Cairo: The Palm Press, 2005.

Rizk, Yunan Labib. "Al-Ahram: A Diwan of Contemporary Life (289)." *Al-Ahram Weekly,* 10–16 June 1999.

———. "Spotlight on the Dean," *Al-Ahram Weekly,* 27 January 2000.

———. "Death of an Uncrowned King," *Al-Ahram Weekly,* 11 October 2001.

Sabit, Adel M. *Seventy Centuries of History: People of the River Valley and Land of the Risen Sun.* Cairo: Maged Farag & Adel Sabit, 1993.

El-Shakry, Omnia. "Cairo as Capital of Socialist Revolution?" Diane Singer and Paul Amar, eds. *Cairo Cosmopolitan.* Cairo: The American University in Cairo Press, 2006.

Stewart, Desmond. *Great Cairo: Mother of the World.* Cairo: The American University in Cairo Press, 1996.

Stone, Caroline. "Ibn Khaldun and the Rise and Fall of Empires," *Saudi Aramco World,* September/October 2006.

Warner, Charles Dudley. "1875, My Winter on the Nile, among Mummies and Moslems," *Orient Line Guide: Chapters for Travellers by Sea and by Land.* London: Thomas Cook and Sons, 1890. http://www.travellersinegypt.org/archives/2004/12/hotel_life_at_shepherds.html

Warner, Nicholas. *The True Description of Cairo: A Sixteenth-Century Venetial View.* Oxford: Oxford University Press, 2006.

Williams, John Alden. "Urbanization and Monument Construction in Mamluk Cairo," Oleg Grabar, ed. *Muqarnas II: An Annual on Islamic Art and Architecture.* New Haven: Yale University Press, 1984.

Wescoat, Jim, Jr. "The Islamic Garden: Issues for Landscape Research," *Environmental Design: Journal of the Islamic Environmental Design Research Centre* 1, 1986.

Index

141